THE FEDERATED CITY

St. Martin's Series
in American Politics

THE
FEDERATED
CITY

COMMUNITY CONTROL
IN LARGE CITIES

Joseph F. Zimmerman
State University of New York at Albany

ST. MARTIN'S PRESS • NEW YORK

For Margaret and Deirdre

Preface

It is a well-publicized fact that in many cities citizen discontent with municipal government has been growing markedly over recent years. This discontent seems to be the product, at least in part, of the development of a ponderous municipal bureaucracy that has slowed down the administrative decision-making process; the unrepresentativeness of city councils and of school boards elected at-large; and the inability of traditional municipal institutions in general to solve the multitudinous problems of large cities. Increasingly, the residents of central cities—particularly those living in disadvantaged neighborhoods —have become alienated from their local governments, which they perceive as being unable and perhaps unwilling to meet citizen needs. And many have become convinced that they are being shortchanged by a closed decision-making process.

The growth of political alienation in our central cities has profound implications for the system of urban government. Although many citizens have "given up" and withdrawn completely from participation in municipal affairs, others—beginning in the mid-sixties—have launched a movement aimed at restructuring the system in such a manner that alienation would be dissipated, popular participation in local government would be maximized, and municipal institutions would be more responsive to the special needs of the disadvantaged. This movement, which seeks to redistribute political power through the creation of a system of neighborhood governments, is the focal point of the present book.

Chapter 1 examines the origins of the neighborhood government movement, the rationale of its proponents, the sketchy model that has been developed, the difficulties encountered in attempting to delineate neighborhood boundaries, and the major problems that neighborhood governments would face.

Actual experience with the type of neighborhood government demanded by the new breed of reformers in large cities has thus far been restricted to community school districts in New York City and Detroit. Chapter 2 is devoted to the politics of establishing a system of limited neighborhood control of schools in these two cities.

The administrative response of large municipal governments to the growing pressures for neighborhood government and a larger role for neighborhoods in the policy formation process is the focus of Chapter 3. Particular attention is paid to innovative attempts to improve neighborhood-city hall communications—by means of complaint bureaus and complaint telephone numbers, neighborhood city halls, police-community relations programs, special neighborhood meetings sponsored by the city government, popularly elected neighborhood councils—and to decentralize administrative functions. To a large extent, these attempts may be collectively labeled a counter reorganization movement, because they are a reaction to the municipal reform movement, launched in the 1890's, which placed a premium upon integration of administrative authority under a strong chief executive, professionalism, and an expanded role for the expert.

Chapter 4 accepts the premise that alienation can be the product of an unrepresentative electoral system as well as the product of failures in city hall-neighborhood communications and in the delivery of municipal services on the neighborhood level. The popularity in ghetto areas of the colonial analogy—which holds that the central business district exploits the other city neighborhoods—is explained primarily in terms of the failures of the at-large electoral system, a product of the municipal reform movement, to provide direct representation for these areas on the city council and school board. Alternative electoral systems—ward elections, combination ward and at-large elections, limited voting, cumulative voting, and proportional representation—are examined in an effort to determine their effectiveness in producing truly representative city councils and school boards.

The concluding chapter suggests that large city governments in the United States can be revitalized by converting the existing unitary system into a federation, improving city hall-neighborhood communications, decentralizing delivery of certain services by the municipal government, and adopting proportional representation. The arguments for and against each element in the reform model are assessed, and the political support for the changes suggested is analyzed.

Mayors and other public officials in large cities supplied the author with much of the data contained in Chapter 3. Additional data on the administrative response to pressures for the creation of a system of neighborhood governments became available in early 1972 with the publication of the results of a survey of cities over 25,000 conducted by Dr. Carl W. Stenberg of the Advisory Commission on Intergovernmental Relations in cooperation with the International City Management Association.

It is impossible to acknowledge individually the hundreds of individuals who have cooperated with the author, yet a debt of gratitude must be expressed to three persons for their suggestions for the improvement of this book: my colleague Ronald M. Stout, George H. Hallett, Jr., of the Citizens Union, and Carl W. Stenberg of the Advisory Commission on Intergovernmental Relations. I would also like to thank Nancy Masterson, whose editing greatly improved the readability of this book, and Edith Connelly, who typed the manuscript.

J.F.Z.

Delmar, New York
September 1972

Contents

NEIGHBORHOOD POLITY

The emergence of the neighborhood government movement in several large American cities was one of the most significant political developments during the decade of the sixties. Supporters of the movement advocate the redistribution of political power by the establishment of a federated city. The present city government would be retained to handle functions most suitable for performance on a city-wide basis (such as water supply, sewage treatment, and refuse disposal), whereas newly created neighborhood governments would be responsible for functions closest to the people (such as schools, libraries, health services, neighborhood parks, and day-care programs).

Agitation for the creation of a system of neighborhood governments has for the most part been concentrated in black ghettos, where the failure of city governments to provide needed facilities and quality services has been most notable. Many alienated* ghetto residents have become convinced that they are being short-changed by a closed decision-making process and believe that a system of neighborhood governments would make the process a more open one.

The growth of citizen interest in neighborhood government (or micro-government) gained impetus following the civil disorders of the mid-1960's, which dramatized the multitudinous problems of severely disadvantaged groups and the inability of local governments to respond adequately to the needs of these groups. The catalogue of complaints

---

* We will use the term *alienation* to mean citizen perceptions that city government is unrepresentative and unresponsive and that the average person is powerless to influence significantly the policy-making process. Central to the concept of alienation are citizen feelings of political impotence and distrust of public officials.

in ghetto areas—deplorable housing conditions, lack of adequate trash and garbage collection, decrepit and poorly staffed schools, high food prices, "police brutality," inadequate recreational facilities, and so forth—is a long one. Private housing is being constructed chiefly for middle- and upper-income families, and public housing has been inadequate in meeting the needs of the poor; to cite only one example, it is estimated that nearly 800,000 housing units for low-income families are needed in New York City alone. The failure of the public school system to properly educate severely disadvantaged children has added to the ferment about community control of schools—an organizational change that proponents maintain will produce a more adequate education for children and restore public confidence in the system. And a Federal Trade Commission study in 1969 found food prices in slum-area supermarkets, because of the lack of competition, to be as much as 10 percent higher than in the same chains' outlets located in middle-class areas. The apparent inability of local governments to deal effectively with such problems has resulted from a number of factors, including the failure of most cities to make institutional changes—administrative and electoral—to cope with urban decay and the changing socioeconomic makeup of their populations.

The rapid development of suburbia since 1945 has had a debilitating effect upon older cities. As members of the white middle class— and with them industry—have moved to outlying areas in increasing numbers, the central cities have lost a substantial part of their tax base while, at the same time, experiencing an influx of low-income persons, both black and white, who have made the welfare rolls swell. During the decade of the 1960's, the white population of central cities decreased by 2.5 million persons. During the same period, 3.4 million blacks moved to central cities, producing a black majority in four large cities—Atlanta, Gary, Newark, and Washington, D.C.—and increasing the black population to over 40 percent in eight others— Baltimore, Birmingham, Detroit, Jackson, Miss., New Orleans, Richmond, Savannah, and St. Louis. The 1970 census showed that one third of the black population in the United States lived in only fifteen cities and that half lived in fifty cities. By and large, city governments have failed to meet the needs of their changed populations or even to establish effective links of communication.

Milton Kotler, a leading advocate of neighborhood governments, contends that the riots in black neighborhoods during the sixties were essentially political events reflecting the establishment of community power in conflict with the established city power and carrying a message—"self-rule."[1] And he adds:

The absolute rule of Negro communities by outside forces has reached the highest degree possible without precipitating rebellion. At the point when practically all decisions affecting public life are made on the outside, a politically confident and conscious people, aspiring to be free, must insist upon a share in local rule.[2]

Regardless of whether one agrees with Kotler's assessment, it is apparent that we do not have government by consent of the governed in many neighborhoods in large cities. Although dissatisfaction is by no means limited to the ghettos, it clearly is concentrated there. A significant number of ghetto residents are openly hostile to the city government, and tension runs high as the more militant view their neighborhoods as "occupied territory." Rhetoric flows freely with shouts of "power to the people," "black power," and "community control." According to Kotler, popularly elected neighborhood governments would be viewed as legitimate by residents in all neighborhoods, including ghettos, and would be in a position to dissipate the discontent which has periodically erupted into civil disorders.

Even in the absence of racial tensions, there would still be ample evidence of the need for new governmental institutions on the local level to meet changing problems and needs and to strengthen citizen involvement. Two of the most prominent organizations concerned with municipal reform, the Committee for Economic Development and the National Commission on Urban Problems, have urged the consolidation of units of local government to form larger units, but they recognize at the same time the need for a mechanism to ensure that neighborhoods will be able to influence policy making. Thus, while recommending an 80 percent reduction in the number of local governments, the Committee for Economic Development (CED) conceded that the sense of community is diminishing and that there is a need for popular participation on the neighborhood level. To guarantee that the distinctive needs of neighborhoods receive proper consideration by the consolidated government, CED in 1966 urged the creation of neighborhood districts of approximately 50,000 population and the election of councils, financed by the consolidated government, to study neighborhood problems, suggest solutions, and voice neighborhood views. CED added that "in some instances, as in the employment of recreation directors, these 'neighborhood councils' might be empowered to take direct action."[3] In 1970, CED recommended a two-tier system of government for metropolitan areas. A new upper tier would be created to perform metropolitan functions, and existing municipalties would function as neighborhood governments.[4] In other words, a system of neighborhood government would be created without breaking up a large city. This proposal, however, does not satisfy individuals who favor the establishment of neighborhood governments *within* a city.

The Royal Commission on Local Government in England recommended in 1969 a vast consolidation of governments outside of the greater London area. The 1,210 existing units would be amalgamated to form fifty-eight single-tier units with populations ranging from 250,000 to 1,000,000, and a two-tier system would be established in three areas of great size and complexity: Birmingham, Liverpool, and Manchester. Although the plan provides for centralization of authority in a smaller number of units of local government, the plan also provides for local councils that would be responsible for rallying and representing neighborhood views before higher authorities.[5] The so-called "main authorities" would be obliged to consult a local council prior to initiating action affecting its area. Representing local views would be the only mandatory function imposed upon the councils. They would, however, be authorized to supplement the amenities furnished by "main authorities" by providing facilities and services designed to promote local convenience, such as parking facilities and street cleaning.

A similar approach could be adopted in large cities in the United States. Neighborhoods could be authorized to elect councils to represent the views of their constituents before the mayor and city council and to determine whether city services should be supplemented by neighborhood services. The supplemental services might be financed by piggybacking a neighborhood tax on the city tax. Serious consideration is being given to a plan of this nature by a temporary commission, created by the 1971 state legislature, to make a study of the governmental operations of New York City.

Federal Promotion of Citizen Participation

The contemporary movement for neighborhood government and greater citizen involvement in municipal affairs has in some measure grown out of increased municipal dependence upon federal funds—currently one fifth of the expense budget in some large cities—and the conditions attached to certain federal grant-in-aid programs, notably the requirement that the citizens affected by the programs be allowed to participate in their planning and/or implementation. Federal promotion of citizen participation in the 1960's undoubtedly contributed to the growing citizen restlessness in ghetto areas and the demand for neighborhood control of programs.

The Urban Renewal Program. The Housing Act of 1954 was the first major law enacted by Congress to promote citizen participation in cities. It requires a municipality, as a condition for the receipt of federal funds, to develop a seven-element "Workable Program" for urban renewal. One of the elements is "citizen participation." This requirement is officially described by the Department of Housing and Urban Development (HUD) as "the keystone of a community's Workable Program" because participation enables citizens to inform themselves of community needs, assist in the development of improvement goals, and learn the means by which the goals can be achieved. According to HUD, citizen participation serves the additional purpose of facilitating the infusion of private resources into a project.

In the early years of the program, local renewal agencies made few serious attempts to generate active citizen participation and support in project areas. Too often little more than lip service was paid to the requirement, and the renewal authority met the letter of the law by forming a citizens' committee which usually played a very limited role in the renewal process. Lacking staff, the committee as a general rule could do little more than react to the plans prepared by the professional staff of the renewal agency. Not uncommonly, the committee was a "blue ribbon" one composed exclusively of prominent individuals, and residents of the project area had no direct representation. Only occasionally was a resident appointed to a subcommittee or a special committee on minority housing. Where residents were involved in early project committees, either they were appointed because they were friendly to the local administration, or an attempt was made to coopt them—that is, to secure their commitment and support for programs developed by the bureaucracy. Consequently, many viewed the "Workable Program" requirement as a cooptative device for manipulating citizens. In spite of the criticisms directed against it, the federal urban renewal program in its early years promoted the organization of neighborhood associations in many cities and in the 1960's formulated more stringent requirements stressing that participation is a device to facilitate residents' contributions to projects rather than a mechanism to achieve resident consensus in support of the project.

HUD's guidelines currently require the establishment of a Project Area Committee composed of residents of the area. The committee must be involved in the planning and administration of social and rehabilitation surveys, establishment of training programs in property management for residents, and relocation surveys and services. An existing neighborhood organization may qualify as the Project Area Committee provided it represents "a fair cross section of the residents." The guidelines also state that there should be a subcommittee on minority housing and that both the committee and subcommittee should include representatives of minority groups. HUD, however, has made clear that the program must be in the firm control of elected officials and that they cannot delegate their responsibility for decision making.

The Antipoverty Program. The antipoverty program, launched by the Economic Opportunity Act of 1964 to raise 35 million persons above the poverty level, marked the beginning of a drastic change in the federal government's attitude toward citizen participation. Bureaucratic democratization was to be fostered to make existing institutions more responsive to the special needs of the poor. In addition to being consulted, citizens were to be given major roles in planning and decision making, including the shifting of resources to meet the needs they perceived to be critical. The act's mandate of "maximum feasible participation of the poor" in the development, coordination, and administration of the poverty program was a revolutionary concept in the minds of most local administrators in 1964, though in accordance with our democratic traditions.

Sargent Shriver, the first Director of the Office of Economic Opportunity, called welfare without representation "tyranny," stressed that "the concept of maximum feasible participation by the poor is an evolutionary one," and stated that no single blueprint for participation could be imposed. He did suggest seven channels of involvement for the poor: employment in antipoverty jobs, education of the poor to be community leaders, service on policy committees, special training and placement programs, carefully supervised work experience coupled with formal instruction and psychological counseling, stimulation of self-help efforts by the poor, and encouragement of the formation of neighborhood organizations in poverty areas.

The new role for the poor citizen mandated by the Economic Opportunity Act highlighted the continuing conflict between participatory democracy and representative democracy. Citizen involvement in the Community Action Program (CAP), it was believed, would bring a new perspective, based upon reality, to problem solving. This involvement would also help humanize the operations of agencies controlled by middle-class white bureaucrats and afford the poor the opportunity to help themselves. The drafters of the clause were displeased by what they considered to be the unresponsiveness of public and private welfare agencies and their paternalistic attitudes which resulted in planning "for" rather than "with" people. The clause was also supported by those convinced that the poor must become politically involved because their interests were not being properly represented by other groups. Only federal funds, the argument went, could ensure the creation of effective new political organizations of the poor.

The local Community Action Agency (CAA) was to be a new urban institution jointly controlled by the poor, public officials, and private organizations. Its objective was the concentration of federal, state, local, and private resources in a coordinated attack on poverty.

Experience indicates that the drafters of the Economic Opportunity Act apparently did not fully recognize the magnitude of the task of coordination being assigned to the CAAs and the possibility that many local CAAs would be more concerned with confrontation—challenging the status quo—and improved delivery of services than with coordination.

As anticipated, mayors generally were opposed to having the poor play a major role in the development and administration of the Community Action Program. Fears developed that new political organizations, funded by the program, might develop into political rivals to the mayor and prepare politically embarrassing demands—integrated housing, for example. Furthermore, the mayor's political position would be enhanced if he controlled the program.

In the early days of the program, mayors of large cities appointed few poor persons to the boards of directors of the local CAA. The federal Office of Economic Opportunity, however, refused to continue funding proposals approved by a CAA lacking members who were poor. Mayors, in consequence, were forced to appoint representatives of the poor to the boards of these agencies. The mayors, however, were able to maintain control since representatives of the poor were in a distinct minority on the board, seldom accounting for one third of the total membership, and the representatives selected were, of course, generally individuals friendly to the mayor.

In 1966, Congress amended the Economic Opportunity Act by stipulating that a minimum of one third of the members of CAA boards must be representatives of the poor who are to be "selected by the residents of the areas of concentration of poverty, with special emphasis on participation by the residents of the area who are poor." Though participation in elections to select representatives of the poor has been small —less than 5 percent of all those eligible and only 0.7 percent in Los Angeles—this level of participation should not be evaluated on the basis of unrealistic standards. The poor have been rebuffed so often that self-defeating attitudes prevail, and it is difficult to convince them that they should participate in the new program.

In late 1967, Congress, at the urging of a number of big city mayors, passed the Green Amendment removing the "maximum feasible participation clause" from the law and stipulating that a local government could either become the CAA or designate an organization to fill the role. Approximately 80 percent of the agencies at the time were private, and 96.7 percent of the local governments elected to continue with the existing agency. The total membership of a CAA board may not number more than fifty-one and must be divided equally among representatives of the poor, elected officials, and individuals representing community organizations. The law is silent relative to whether the board is to control the CAA or simply be an advisory body.

The Community Action Program promoted the organization of neighborhood service centers staffed by state and local officials responsible for code enforcement, public health, public welfare, employment, and other functions. By 1968, an estimated eight hundred centers were in operation. The program also created neighborhood advisory councils—approximately one thousand by 1968—to convey views to the neighborhood centers and the city-wide CAA. A number of advisory councils have been converted into neighborhood corporations responsible for CAA functions in their areas. These corporations, which may be viewed as a limited form of neighborhood government, are discussed later in this chapter.

The antipoverty program promoted citizen organization in low-income neighborhoods and led to the political mobilization of the poor against officialdom. Not surprisingly, the program became the subject of considerable controversy in many cities as a power struggle developed between the "establishment" and organizations of the poor. Poverty funds were utilized for political purposes, such as registering voters, organizing protest marches on city hall, and launching vigorous attacks on welfare departments and school boards in particular. This type of militant action and the employment of emotional confrontation rhetoric proved vexatious to most public officials and many citizens and induced Congress to alter the enabling act in 1967 by means of the Green Amendment. Poverty personnel and funds cannot be utilized to register voters, and poverty personnel in the performance of their duties are precluded from participating "in any form of picketing, protest, or other direct action which is in violation of the law." In other words, CAAs no longer are allowed to clash with the establishment and function as pressure groups.

The full impact of the antipoverty program on urban society in general is still being debated. Nevertheless, we can conclude without fear of contradiction that the program promoted the mobilization of the political power of the poor and the articulation of dissatisfaction at the grass-roots level, led to confrontation politics as political activists took over a number of local CAAs, and increased the demand for effective citizen participation in governmental programs and community control of programs. As indigenous leadership developed, citizens in many poverty neighborhoods began to recognize that they could organize successfully and prod city agencies into being more responsive.

The Model Cities Program. A third federal program premised upon active citizen involvement is the Model Cities program authorized by the Demonstration Cities and Metropolitan Development Act of 1966. Conceived as an innovative neighborhood program, it was initially limited to an area not exceeding 10 percent of the total area of a city. The size restriction was removed in 1969, and the program now can cover an entire city. To encourage experimentation, communities selected to participate in the program receive a supplemental "bloc" grant of 80 percent of the nonfederal share of regular categorical grants-in-aid received under the program.

The purpose of the program, currently limited to 150 cities, is the mobilization of public and private resources in a comprehensive and coordinated effort to solve the economic, physical, and social problems of blighted neighborhoods by facilitating the participation of Model Cities residents. During the first year, participating cities were directed to prepare a five-year program and to "chronicle the methods and approaches used to achieve widespread citizen participation, and the relationship between the views of the citizens and the various elements of the model neighborhood plan."

Although the city government is legally responsible for the program, residents of the target neighborhood are to have a significant role in planning and conducting the program. Particular stress is placed upon the involvement of local residents with the public and private agencies needed to carry out the program. All federal funds in support of a Model Cities project are channeled directly to the municipal government and not to organizations of residents. A number of cities, though, have contracted with citizen organizations for planning studies and have supplied grants to pay for their staff and consultants.

The basic statutory requirement for "widespread citizen participation" has been interpreted by HUD to mean that municipal officials must work closely with Model Cities residents throughout the formulation and implementation phases of the program by maintaining a continuing dialogue. HUD neither specifies the ideal form of citizen participation nor specifies a method for the selection of citizens to represent the model neighborhood. HUD, however, has established performance standards for citizen participation that must be met by each City Demonstration Agency (CDA). The stated objective is to develop a structure of representation that makes cooptation impossible and ensures that the program is developed and implemented cooperatively by the city government and the residents of the project area.

A new or existing citizen organization may meet HUD's performance standards provided the leadership of the organization is composed of individuals "whom neighborhood residents accept as representing their interests." Furthermore, the citizen participation structure must be provided with technical assistance and have direct access to the CDA's decision-making process in order to be in a position to influence planning and program decisions. Nearly all Model Cities programs are located in the target areas of the Community Action Program, and there has been considerable cooperation between the two programs, including the CDA's delegation of certain planning and organizing functions to the CAA.

Approximately fifty of the first seventy-five "first-round" Model Cities held elections to select neighborhood representatives. Cambridge, Massachusetts, had a 40 percent turnout of eligible residents, Winston-Salem a 29 percent turnout, Toledo 25 percent, and Dayton 24 percent. In several cities, militants, expressing the fear that the CDA would attempt to coopt them, boycotted the election and later charged that the citizen organization was unrepresentative. A second group of cities invited existing neighborhood organizations to appoint representatives to an official neighborhood coalition, and a third group of cities relied upon the mayor or CDA director to appoint neighborhood leaders. A few cities used a combined election and appointment system.'

Early in the Model Cities program, HUD officials stressed there was to be a partnership arrangement between city officials and neighborhood residents. The program was launched during the Johnson administration without full clarification of the nature of "widespread citizen participation." In a number of cities, Model Cities residents assumed that they would control the program, and the local administration acquiesced. With the advent of the Nixon administration, HUD began to insist that city hall must exercise final authority over the program with the role of the citizen limited to assistance in planning, coordinating, monitoring, and evaluating the program.

The change in the officially prescribed role for citizens has led many neighborhood leaders to charge that the Model Cities program is a fraud perpetrated against the poor because citizen participation has become more of a ritual than a reality. An air of cynicism and disillusionment in a number of cities has replaced initial citizen expectations that the program would have a significant impact in improving conditions in ghetto areas. Alienation has been increasing between city hall and disadvantaged neighborhoods in most large cities, and federal insistence that the Model Cities program be municipally controlled appears to be increasing the pressure for neighborhood government in large cities. This is most likely to occur if the city coopts the neighborhood organization or it loses its representativeness.

The Model Cities program has been recommended by Sundquist and Davis as the best structure for program planning and coordination in urban ghettos. The CAAs, in the opinion of Sundquist and Davis, demonstrate that the planning and coordinating functions are incompatible with the responsibility for operating programs.[6] In contrast to the CAA, the CDA was designed to be a public agency responsible to local elected officials with provision for "widespread citizen participation." These agencies undoubtedly will lose their potential as coordinators if they come under resident control and function as advocate planners, because they would offend public and private social welfare organizations. It is unlikely that Sundquist and Davis' suggestion that the CDA help neighborhood organizations develop an adequate staff will satisfy the more militant neighborhood leaders.

The newness of the Model Cities program makes the rendering of a judgment of its impact on neighborhoods difficult. It appears to be safe to conclude, however, that the program's impact on neighborhood politics will be minimal in comparison to the impact made by the antipoverty program during its early years.

Neighborhood Government

Local government has been highly praised as grass-roots government close to the people, but this is not the situation in most large cities today. The growth of a ponderous bureaucracy has slowed down the administrative decision-making process, and traditional municipal institutions have been unable to cope with the varying problems found in different neighborhoods. As a result, many citizens have become alienated from their local government; they feel that the city government is unrepresentative and unresponsive and that the average person is powerless to influence the policy-making process in any significant way. A sense of helplessness pervades their neighborhoods. A great many citizens have withdrawn from participation in the political system. Others have demanded major institutional changes aimed at giving neighborhoods a greater voice in determining policy. Agitation has not occurred in all neighborhoods, nor has it been uniform in the neighborhoods where it has arisen. In one neighborhood residents may wish to control schools, for example, and in another they may primarily want to control the police.

The prescription for more responsive government offered by reformers today varies considerably from relatively minor structural and procedural changes, to the creation of a federation within the city, to the complete replacement of the city government by neighborhood governments. The latter is based upon a concept that is in accordance with American political traditions favoring citizen participation and training, decentralization of authority, and small units of government.

The current interest in neighborhood government reflects a desire for access to the government by reducing the geographical scale of local government and for a return to participatory democracy as epitomized by the New England town meeting. Kotler asks: "Can't the residents and mothers of the neighborhood determine the kind of day-care program that best fits the community? The same can also be said of recreation, libraries, schools, health, welfare, and so forth. What does a community gain in the unitary centralized control of these programs by a central structure of some millions of people?"[7]

Neighborhood government means "control" or "control-sharing" and must be contrasted with locally sponsored citizen-participation programs on the neighborhood level that are advisory in nature and often little more than symbolic. In many cities, "citizen participation" has taken the form of officials notifying neighborhood residents of plans for municipal projects. More recently, as we have seen, officials have made a serious attempt to consult residents on a give-and-take basis relative to proposed improvements and programs. However, "citizen participation"—whether it be in the form of providing information or consultation—does not satisfy the proponents of neighborhood government who insist that a fundamental change in the decision-making process within cities is essential. The most alienated citizens view officially sponsored citizen-participation programs as cooptation—that is, a process to secure the commitment and support of citizens for programs developed by the bureaucracy. Power is not shared, and citizen participation is designed merely to give legitimacy to a program.

The theoretical concept of neighborhood government is based on the federalist model and is traceable to Thomas Jefferson's "republics-in-miniature." In a letter to John Adams, dated October 28, 1813, Jefferson suggested the division of counties into "wards"; each would be self-governing with respect to such functions as the militia, police, roads, welfare, and minor judicial cases. Other functions could be added, according to Jefferson, provided they could be better managed by the "wards" than by the county or state. Although Jefferson was referring to agricultural communities and not to large cities, his views merit re-examination in the light of the serious difficulties our largest cities currently are experiencing in their attempts to adapt and respond to the widely differing problems and needs of various neighborhoods.

Neighborhood government is not a new concept. We have had a great deal of experience, though generally unrecognized, with it. Suburban governments are viewed as neighborhood governments by many residents of black ghettos, who assert that they should be able to control the institutions of government in their neighborhoods in a manner similar to white control of governmental institutions in suburbia, from which most blacks, for a variety of reasons, are effectively excluded. If one does not accept the contention that suburban governments are genuine neighborhood governments, one must concede that incorporated urban villages located within sections of suburban towns, as in New York State, and multifunctional special districts within towns may properly be considered genuine neighborhood governments. Incorporated villages are municipalities and typically possess powers similar to those possessed by cities.

Citizen organization on the neighborhood level in middle-class areas has long been a fact of political life in our cities and may be viewed as an informal and extralegal system of neighborhood government. To cite only one example, New York City for many years has had active block and civic associations in the west and upper west sides of Manhattan as well as political clubs active in servicing neighborhood needs. The objectives of these associations are many and varied—elimination of health, fire, and safety hazards; repair or demolition of abandoned buildings; enforcement of codes by city officials; public support for city programs designed to improve neighborhood conditions; relocation of tenants displaced by public projects; traffic control; improved playground facilities; and other civic and social programs. Middle-class neighborhood associations often contract for services not provided by the city, such as rubbish collection, and operate parks and swimming pools. In addition, an increasing number of associations contract for private police protection to supplement municipal police protection. In a few cities—Minneapolis, Minnesota, and Worcester, Massachusetts, for example—the associations have banded together in a city-wide organization. These neighborhood associations, however, have not demanded independence, total or partial, from the city.

Growing Support for Neighborhood Government. Popular interest in the organization of neighborhood governments developed primarily in black ghettos as the political consciousness of blacks was stimulated by the civil rights and antipoverty programs during the 1960's. Although no comprehensive survey of black support for the establishment of a system of neighborhood governments has been undertaken, we can conclude with reasonable confidence that such support is growing, as evidenced by an important change in the thinking of a growing number of black leaders. Until recently black leaders had been working in the civil rights movement to achieve integration of the races; today, many of them have abandoned integration as a goal for achieving equal opportunity and are pressing for black separatism.

Some blacks are convinced that a system of neighborhood government, which would allow blacks and whites to control institutions in their respective neighborhoods, is more politically acceptable to the dominant white majority than total integration. In his study of the black demand for community control, Alan A. Altshuler maintains that "white resistance to massive desegregation and redistribution is overwhelming, and it comes from all segments of white society. The resistance to community control, by contrast, is centered in the big city public bureaucracies."[8] A second group of leaders—who are a type of black nationalist—holds that black culture is superior to white culture and that efforts to achieve integration are misdirected. Other black nationalists hold that the contributions of black culture have been underemphasized. Still other black leaders are convinced that it is easier to mobilize the political power of blacks if they are geographically concentrated and that such mobilization will facilitate their acquiring political experience. In a sense, separation of the races in the form of neighborhood governments may be viewed as a form of segregation that is legitimized.

The Congress of Racial Equality (CORE) in 1970 abandoned its long-sought goal of integration by endorsing a public school plan based upon "desegregation without integration"—a plan favored by many whites. CORE believed this new plan was a more feasible approach to the solution of racial problems because it provided for black control of the "instruments of power" in their neighborhoods. Under the CORE plan, the neighborhood school concept would be preserved, and children would be allowed to freely transfer to other school districts. Other civil rights organizations, however, such as the National Association for the Advancement of Colored People (NAACP), still adhere to the credo of school integration as the best technique for achieving racial equality.

In 1970, the Congress of African People called for local control of the instruments of government, including the hiring and firing of policemen and the establishment of a neighborhood security force. The National Committee to Combat Fascism, sponsored by the Black Panthers, successfully utilized initiative petitions to place on the April 6, 1971, ballot in Berkeley, California, a proposal for community control of police; the proposal was defeated by a vote of 22,712 to 16,142. Under the plan, the city would have been divided into "black," "campus," and "white" communities. Each community would have elected an autonomous police council with complete responsibility for all police activities. All policemen would have been required to be residents of the community, for it was believed that police harassment of community residents would be reduced if policemen would know the culture of the community and develop a sense of "oneness." The council also would have been authorized to establish other requirements for the appointment of policemen. Opponents of the plan charged it would "be an invitation to chaos" and create three "de facto sub-governments" in place of a unified municipality.

The New Reformers. A new breed of reformer, who appeared on the municipal scene in the 1960's, contends that institutional arrangements have stressed the wrong values. The new reformers charge that too much emphasis has been placed upon centralization of power in city hall, professionalism, and economy and efficiency, while too little attention has been paid to responsiveness as a criterion of democratic government. They also maintain that the supercentralization of power in city hall, development of uniform city-wide policies which ignore unique conditions in certain areas of the city, and growth of a ponderous bureaucracy are responsible for neighborhood-city hall alienation and for the failure of city governments to solve the most pressing urban problems. The growing popularity of the concept of neighborhood government is a reaction against a professionalized and specialized bureaucracy insulated from citizens and to some extent from elected officials. Consumers of municipal services often resent the patronizing attitude of "expert administrators" and feel that as citizens they have no voice in determining the policy of the administering agency—which appears to be a fiefdom—because they are excluded from the centers of decision making.

Reformers urging the creation of neighborhood governments preach a type of political fundamentalism and argue that large units of government do not necessarily plan better, achieve a higher level of service and more economies, or tax more equitably than small units. Nor do economies of scale, according to the reformers, have to be sacrificed in order to achieve responsiveness and to adapt to varying neighborhood conditions. A call is issued for institutional and procedural changes, including neighborhood government, which putatively will maximize citizen participation and governmental responsiveness to the special needs of individual neighborhoods. The argument is advanced that concentration of power in city hall is no longer the proper prescription for the ills of cities. Political realities necessitate a new organizational accommodation and a major redistribution of power and resources to produce institutions sensitive to local needs, to restore a sense of community, and to meet the needs of neighborhoods by ensuring that policies are determined with neighborhood inputs. Such a redistribution will revitalize decision-making processes and invigorate citizen participation.

The new populists contend that the grass-roots citizenry has the capacity to make proper decisions, often superior to those made by professional bureaucrats, and that it is a cruel system which deprives citizens of the privilege of making mistakes and learning from them. Furthermore, neighborhood government is inherently good because it maximizes *vox populi*, and residents will acquire a "stake" in the governmental system by exercising control over the delivery of services. Alienated citizens are convinced that bureaucratic institutions are incapable of reforming themselves and that only citizens are capable of instituting needed governmental reforms. Furthermore, it is contended that citizens will perceive the elected officials of neighborhood governments as more approachable and responsive than professional bureaucrats operating out of city hall. Altshuler writes,that community control "would give blacks a tangible stake in the American political system. By giving them systems they considered their own, it would—hopefully —enhance the legitimacy of the whole system in their eyes."[9]

The new reformers differ sharply with the views of the early twentieth-century reformers who were interested in cleaning up corruption and creating a city government capable of providing services in the most economical and efficient manner. The early reformers generally were successful in achieving their objectives; yet they set the stage for a new era of reform because of their overemphasis upon economy, efficiency, and professionalism and their failure to ensure that the new governmental institutions would be sufficiently responsive to the needs of disadvantaged citizens. The new urban critics maintain that the old-style civic reformers tend to be elitist and are out of touch with political realities and that the oligarchs, produced by the early reform movement, must be replaced. In many instances, this would mean the return of certain functions to neighborhoods which were municipalities prior to their annexation to the central city in the nineteenth and early twentieth centuries.

Most of the new reformers are not advocating secession of neighborhoods from the city but rather partial disannexation of neighborhoods, as a counterweight to central power, to ensure that those who have been left out of the political decision-making system are given a role to play. Kotler urges the establishment of a federation involving a new spatial distribution of governmental power. Certain powers would be possessed exclusively by either the city government or the neighborhood governments while other powers would be shared. The present city government would be responsible for functions that must be handled on a broad geographical basis, such as water supply and sewage disposal. Newly created neighborhood governments, governed by town meetings, would handle the functions closest to the people, such as schools, police, and health services. A neighborhood government's control over these functions would not be reviewable by the city. However, a neighborhood government could adopt the "Lakewood Plan" and contract with the city for the performance of one or more functions in the same manner that cities in Los Angeles County voluntarily obtain services from the county on a contract basis to take advantage of economies of scale. Since neighborhood governments would determine the type and level of services they wish to perform, diversity in terms of the provision of services would be common among neighborhoods. This is a typical feature of a federated system.

Proponents of a federated city have not yet prepared a detailed model, and their writings generally fail to indicate the procedure for determining neighborhood boundaries, the method of financing the governments, the precise division of powers between the city and neighborhood governments, and the organization of the upper and lower tiers of government. They do, however, make clear that their proposal involves the creation of neighborhood governments with complete responsibility for specific functions indefinitely—an *imperium in imperio*.

The Federated City. The federated city might be organized on the model found in the Toronto area, where the governing body of the upper tier or metropolitan government is composed of the mayor, reeves, and other elected officials of the city of Toronto and five boroughs. The council of a federated city could be composed of *ex officio* officials—the chief executive officers and presidents of neighborhood councils. And the city-wide board of education could be composed of the chairmen of community school boards. Such an approach might have the advantages of lessening neighborhood-city hall conflict, allowing neighborhoods to influence city-wide policy more effectively, and creating a more representative council. This approach, unfortunately, would suffer the disadvantages associated with the traditional ward elected council, including logrolling, which might result in the neglect of city-wide concerns. Each member would be similar to a delegate to an international conference and probably would seek to further the interests of his neighborhood. Although the United States Supreme Court's one-man, one-vote doctrine probably has made the metropolitan Toronto approach unworkable in the United States—since neighborhood governments would have to be of substantially equal populations—a scheme of weighted voting might be developed which could be in conformance with the Court's dicta. However, boundary lines would have to be redrawn or the number of votes assigned to each member would have to be changed at least decennially to reflect population shifts.

Recognizing the potential of conflict between city hall and neighborhoods attempting to protect what they consider to be their rights, the Advisory Commission on Intergovernmental Relations (ACIR) added to its proposal for neighborhood subunits of governments a provision that the subunits could be unilaterally dissolved by the city.[10] Viewing this proposal as tokenism and a cooptative device, proponents of autonomous neighborhood governments state that the dissolution of a subunit during a period of controversy would completely rupture neighborhood-city hall communications and might precipitate civil disorders. An alternative to dissolving a subunit would be the city government's retention of the power to revoke the subunit's right to perform a disputed function. In other words, the city would retain the power of preemption but would lack the power to dissolve the neighborhood government.

The Neighborhood Corporation

Advocates of neighborhood government agree that local initiative is the proper method for creating new units of government and that state enabling legislation is needed. Citizens should be afforded the opportunity to create such units but should not be forced to accept them if local agreement as to their need is lacking.

Kotler suggests that the private, nonprofit neighborhood corporation, chartered by the state, is the most desirable mechanism for forming a new government and increasing public alertness and popular participation. The neighborhood corporation, it is suggested, will develop realistic local programs and achieve genuine accomplishments since residents know their own needs and the corporation will be able to respond quickly to these needs. Kotler cautions that the transfer of authority cannot be "accomplished overnight." With strong leadership and the passage of time, the corporation will solidify its position in the neighborhood and will be converted into a public corporation.

Kotler's model is the East Central Citizens Organization (ECCO), organized in 1966 in Columbus, Ohio, which operates in a one square mile area with a population of 6,500. The First English Lutheran Church turned its settlement house over to the newly created ECCO, which offers educational, recreational, and youth services; purchases homes for rehabilitation; and operates a credit unit and a veterinary clinic. ECCO's experience, according to Kotler, demonstrates that settlement houses and Office of Economic Opportunity (OEO) funded multiservice centers in many instances can serve as the initial basis for neighborhood governments responsible for a number of social services.

The initiative for the creation of neighborhood or community corporations was provided by the federal Economic Opportunity Act of 1964, and the first ones received antipoverty funds in 1966. Further initiative was provided by the federal Model Cities program during

the latter part of the Johnson administration. Three of the most successful corporations are the Model Urban Neighborhood Development
Corporation in Baltimore, Watts Labor Community Action Committee
in Los Angeles, and Friends of Clinton Hill, Incorporated, in Newark,
New Jersey.

The Model Urban Neighborhood Corporation (MUND) was incorporated in 1967 and is one of the few neighborhood corporations
with an elected board running a community action program in a partnership with private enterprise—the Westinghouse Corporation, Baltimore Electronics, Lions Brothers, and the Greater Baltimore Committee.
During its first three years of operation, MUND received OEO grants
totaling $1,910,000 to continue its innovative development plan. MUND
has assisted over four hundred individuals to find jobs, established a
newspaper, helped persuade the board of education to construct two
new elementary schools, assisted the city in the rehabilitation of a
multipurpose neighborhood center, started a summer recreation program
for children, and helped the department of health initiate a rat control program.

Watts Labor Community Action Committee (WLCAC), organized
in 1965, is one of the most extensive community development operations in the United States, handling millions of dollars in annual income. Composed of three corporations, WLCAC operates a retail super-
market, a housing program, a credit union, a poultry ranch, two service stations, and numerous nonprofit projects.

Friends of Clinton Hill, Incorporated, is an unusual neighborhood
corporation in that it is supported by black residents of the neighborhood and suburban whites. With a board of ten black and ten white
trustees, the corporation operates the Bessie Smith Community Center,
an educational and recreational facility which also operates a dental
clinic one day a week.

The boards of community corporations are usually elected by residents of local poverty areas who are at least eighteen years of age.
Voter turnout has been light, generally less than 5 percent of those
eligible. In New York City the boards of twenty-six such corporations
are elected and are responsible for studying problems and recommending how federal and city funds should be spent for antipoverty programs. Many of these boards are urging that they be recognized as the
basis for a system of neighborhood government.

Howard W. Hallman visited community corporations and unincorporated neighborhood boards in a number of cities and reports
that "residents see the corporations as *theirs,* not as a distant and im-
personal bureaucracy."[11] Yet the question must be asked how many
residents truly view "the corporations as *theirs*" in view of the fact that

resident participation in elections for boards of directors has been less than 5 percent everywhere. Therefore, the representativeness of these boards as well as their accountability must be questioned.

Kotler states that the governing body of a neighborhood corporation should be membership meetings similar to New England town meetings. In recent years, however, the town meeting has been attacked as undemocratic in practice. Citizen apathy is a common charge against town meeting government, and the charge cannot be denied if town meeting attendance in the typical town is an accurate barometer of such apathy. Attendance at the annual meeting which acts on many important subjects, including the town budget, is small unless the warrant (agenda) contains one or more "hot" issues. Formal decisions often are made by less than 10 percent of the registered voters. Attendance at special town meetings is sparse if the warrant contains only routine articles, and a meeting held during the summer months may have to be adjourned for lack of a quorum.

For sundry reasons, a large percentage of registered voters voluntarily abdicate power which is rightfully theirs, and their nonattendance at an open town meeting may be interpreted as a vote of confidence in a *de facto* representative town meeting, which may or may not be truly representative. A *de jure* representative town meeting functions in the same manner as an open town meeting, but only elected town meeting members may vote. Fortunately, attendance appears to be related to the importance of the unresolved issues; apathy disappears when a major issue is brought to the town meeting for resolution. Furthermore, there is little evidence that the *de facto* representative town meeting consistently thwarts the general will.[12]

The clock cannot be turned back to an earlier era, and doubts must be raised relative to the transferability of a governmental institution from one environment to another. The town meeting has been the legislative body of New England towns for nearly 350 years and is deeply rooted in tradition and practice. Yet the meetings have been plagued by the twin problems of poor attendance and relative lack of debate. Will residents of ghetto neighborhoods attend and actively participate in the membership meetings of corporations? Kotler anticipates that participation may only be 10 percent of those eligible, but he defends membership meetings with low participation on the ground that city officials often are elected by the same or smaller percentage of the eligible voters. Experience with poverty elections indicates that participation by more than 5 percent of those eligible is improbable and participation by 2 or 3 percent is more likely. Kotler also justifies the use of the membership meeting on the ground "that it will serve the common interest, not special interests. Lawmaking by an assembly of citizens will favor the many rather than the few, simply because wealth and special interest have a smaller vote in the public assembly than in elected councils."[13] Many political scientists would argue the contrary point, and experience with the New England town meeting indicates that it is the special interests who faithfully attend.

With the exception of the community development corporations engaged in providing job opportunities, neighborhood corporations to date have assumed responsibility only for antipoverty programs financed by the federal government and private agencies. Kotler believes that neighborhood corporations would be the most suitable recipients for power and resources transferred from county and municipal governments. A transfer of power could be made by means of a contract providing for an unreversible delegation, a periodic delegation, or a reversible delegation. Under the first, authority once delegated could not be revoked by the grantor. Under the second, authority would be delegated for a specified period of time and would be subject to renewal upon expiration of the stipulated time period. Reversible delegation— recommended, as we have noted, by the Advisory Council on Intergovernmental Relations—would enable the delegator to withdraw all power at any time by dissolving the neighborhood subunit.

Howard W. Hallman concluded that neighborhood corporations have a spotty record; some have been successful and others are experiencing difficulties in surviving.[14] Success is attributed to the development of community unity and a competent executive director and staff. To date, corporations do not measure up well in terms of accountability, citizen participation, and representativeness. Neighborhood opinion is not always solicited by the corporations, and public hearings usually are not held before decisions are made. It would be a mistake, however, to draw firm conclusions on the limited experience of corporations since the mid-1960's. Success is apt to come incrementally.

Optimum Size. Accepting the desirability of creating neighborhood governments through local initiative, one is confronted with the difficult problem of determining the spatial boundaries of such units. Kotler writes that "the most sensible way to locate the neighborhood is to ask people where it is, for people spend much time fixing its boundaries."[15] He also defines neighborhoods in terms of units of local government annexed to the central city, primarily in the nineteenth century. The Germantown area of Philadelphia and the Roxbury area of Boston are cited as examples of neighborhoods which once were self-governing communities and now are demanding independence from the city. What he fails to note is that the population makeup of these areas has changed considerably. Roxbury was initially inhabited primarily by residents of English descent but now has a predominantly black population. Kotler also suggests that neighborhoods should range in size from 2,500 to 75,000 persons and one half to six square miles in area. Unfortunately, his criteria for determining spatial boundaries by the territorial loyalties of citizens are too general and therefore inadequate.

A political community can be created by the arbitrary drawing of territorial boundary lines, since this would give residents certain common interests, focusing upon the functions allocated to the neighborhood government. A deep-felt sense of community, however, is often difficult to achieve in a day and age of mass communications and mobile citizens, with one family in five moving annually. While the population is relatively stable in many middle-income neighborhoods, population mobility is endemic in ghetto areas. In consequence, a sense of community is more likely to develop in the first type of neighborhood, yet the demand for autonomy does not necessarily correlate with length of residence. In creating a neighborhood government one cannot rely upon people's attachment to their neighbors, for this would result in a population and geographical area too small for most governmental purposes. Reliance on boundary lines perceived by citizens is also an inadequate method because residents in few areas will agree upon the boundaries of their neighborhoods. Natural features, such as a river or a ravine, usually impede communications and, consequently, can serve as a neighborhood boundary; yet sharp divisions may exist within the natural boundaries, and little neighboring may occur.

Although no reliable method has been invented to demarcate neighborhoods, various administrative, economic, and political criteria can be employed to determine the optimum geographical size of a unit of government for the effective performance of specified functions.[16] First, a local government must have the administrative and fiscal capacity to provide quality services. If a unit lacks adequate financial resources, it obviously will be unable to meet the needs of its citizens in a satisfactory manner. A neighborhood government should be authorized to levy user charges and property, income, and sales taxes. These taxes might be collected for the neighborhood government by the city, county, or state. Furthermore, a neighborhood government should not be burdened with restrictive tax and debt limits but should be made eligible to receive federal and state grants-in-aid. Even if these suggestions are adopted, many neighborhoods will lack the fiscal resources to support a neighborhood government unless there is a more general redistribution of income.

Second, cost-benefit analysis can be employed to determine the area which primarily benefits from a service and therefore should be responsible for the provision of that service. Ideally, boundary lines should be drawn in such a manner that there would be as little benefit spillover to other units as possible. Admittedly, it is difficult to identify the spillover of social benefits and costs, and the amount of spillover may vary with different subfunctions. A function may provide direct benefits in a given area and indirect benefits over a much wider area. A major park, for example, will benefit a much wider area than a tot lot.

Third, a minimum and maximum population and geographical area can be employed to determine boundaries. The minimum population should be approximately 25,000 and a population in excess of 250,000 would appear to be too large if relatively close citizen identification with the neighborhood government is to be fostered. Although these criteria are to a large extent arbitrary, the population and geographical area of the government should be sufficient to enable the achievement of economies of scale; unit costs generally decrease with an increase in output. The area, however, should be as compact as possible, with no isolated pockets, and should not be so large that communications are impeded and citizen access to the centers of decision making is limited. The ideal area, of course, will vary from one function to another. A study by the Advisory Commission on Intergovernmental Relations (ACIR) concluded that the size of a city in the population range of 25,000 to 250,000 has no significant relationship to economies or diseconomies of scale, but that the law of diminishing returns applies as size exceeds 250,000, resulting in significant diseconomies of scale.[17] The largest diseconomies are associated with police protection.

Fourth, the government should be multifunctional in order to avoid the fragmentation of responsibility associated with single-purpose agencies, allow for the development of priorities in the allocation of resources within the area, and center public attention on one government.

Fifth, the government should be accountable and accessible to its citizens in such a manner that popular participation is maximized. This means that the unit of government should be small enough to allow citizens to identify with it and permit ready access to elected and appointed officials.

The relative emphasis placed upon a given criterion will influence the determination of the spatial limits of a neighborhood government. Citizens in one region may assign a higher weight to one criterion in comparison to others, and this naturally will affect the geographical area considered to be optimum.

The logical method for determining the most desirable area for the performance of functions is to apply the criteria to each function. Since most functions, such as police administration, involve subfunctions capable of being performed on different territorial bases, the determination of the optimal area for a given function can be difficult. As an illustration, consider the various police activities—crime prevention, criminal identification, traffic control, foot patrol, and motor patrol. Each could be performed ideally in a different geographical area. Criminal identification might best be performed on a statewide basis, traffic control on a metropolitan basis, motor patrol on a city-wide basis, and foot patrol on a neighborhood basis. This, of course, is an argument in favor of shared responsibility for functions and makes interlevel coordination essential. As the ACIR has pointed out, "each function must be viewed from at least four different time phases of administration: planning, decision making, actual administration or execution, and finally, evaluation."[18] Planning for the performance of a function might occur on the metropolitan level, decision making on the city level, and execution on the neighborhood level. Evaluation could occur on each level.

Consideration must also be given to "partnership federalism" as a determinant of the area responsible for the performance of a function or subfunction. Most traditional local governmental functions as well as many newer ones are performed in partnership with the state and federal governments. Each may influence or dictate the geographical area within which a function is to be administered.

Finally, provision must be made for the adjustment of the boundaries of neighborhood governments to cope with changing conditions, for experience has shown that immutable municipal boundaries are undesirable. A boundary commission should be created and authorized to determine the initial boundaries of neighborhood governments and later make adjustments by applying prescribed criteria. Until neighborhood governments are activated, the most feasible method of selecting members to the commission would be appointment by the mayor or city manager. Provision could be made at a later date for neighborhood officials to serve on the commission, except when an official's neighborhood is the subject of commission action.

Finances. Clearly one of the principal obstacles in the path of creating neighborhood governments is finances. Most neighborhood corporations grew out of the federal antipoverty program administered by OEO and, consequently, may be viewed as a federally subsidized form of neighborhood control. To cite two atypical examples, the Model Urban Neighborhood Corporation (MUND) in Baltimore received OEO grants totaling $1,910,000 during its first three years of operation, and the Cleveland Neighborhood Health Service Incorporated received an OEO grant of $1,771,501 to expand comprehensive health care services for the poor. Sharp curtailment of funding for the antipoverty program has greatly weakened neighborhood corporations.

Ghetto neighborhoods lack the fiscal resources to support needed governmental programs, and other units of government—federal, state, county, and city—will be reluctant to fund neighborhood governments unless control is maintained, including the power to terminate funds if they are improperly utilized. Neighborhood governments, of course, can be made eligible for conditional federal and state grants-in-aid and become active partners in a cooperative federal system. The grants-in-aid, among other things, would tend to give legitimacy to the neighborhood governments.

Senator Abraham Ribicoff of Connecticut in 1967 introduced in the United States Senate a bill—S. 1433—providing federal financial support to cover the cost of organizing and operating corporations in neighborhoods with a population between 2,500 and 50,000 for a two-year period. Congress, however, has not approved the bill.

The Advisory Commission on Intergovernmental Relations (AICR) recommends that neighborhood subunits of government be granted a limited power of taxation, "such as a fractional millage on the property tax to be collected by the city or county as a part of the property tax bill and returned to the neighborhood for use as its governing body determines."[19] It is unlikely that cities and towns will adopt this recommendation without attaching strings to the use of the funds. The corporations also could raise funds by selling shares of stock to residents. The sale of shares would serve more as an involvement function than a revenue-raising function since the amount raised by this method in ghetto areas would be miniscule in terms of the amount required to fully fund the corporation and its programs.

The only major exception to the above statement on fund raising by the sale of shares has been Zion Investment Associates, Incorporated, of North Philadelphia, organized in 1962 by the Zion Baptist Church. Each of more than two hundred members of the congregation was persuaded to invest ten dollars per month for thirty-six months to finance a black-owned community corporation. In 1965, four hundred additional parishioners purchased stock, and three years later stock was made available to nonparishioners. By 1970, in excess of $.5 million of capital was raised by the sale of stock. The General Electric Company was persuaded to provide management assistance and a sheltered market by awarding a $2.5 million contract for the purchase of products manufactured by the new corporation. The strong equity position of the corporation facilitated the obtaining of outside capital without restrictions being placed upon the use of the funds. Resident participation in the affairs of the corporation does not approach Kotler's ideal of widespread community participation, however. In 1970, only seven thousand persons—a very small percentage of the community's total black population—owned or were purchasing stock on the installment plan. Few nonparishioners owned shares because they were unable to come up with the ten dollars required for monthly installment payments.

A second exceptional community development corporation is Action Industries, Incorporated, located in the Venice area of Los Angeles. The corporation received a $.5 million no-interest loan and management assistance from Commonwealth United Corporation, a diversified firm, whose president was concerned with the problems of the area. Because of the lack of indigenous leadership, most operating decisions appear to be made by consultants hired by Commonwealth United Corporation, and community participation has been minimal.

Kotler apparently recognizes fully the difficulties that a neighborhood corporation in a ghetto area will experience in obtaining credit, yet he states that the corporation will experience no difficulty in obtaining credit if the corporation is endowed with the power of eminent domain. Kotler's analysis in this case is totally divorced from economic reality. His view of the city's economy is based upon the Marxist concept of economic imperialism—the exploitation of colonies, the neighborhoods, by the mother country, or central business district—and his policy for developing the economy of a disadvantaged neighborhood is based upon mercantilism or economic nationalism. His prescription of local ownership of all industry and commerce within a neighborhood, for example, is completely unrealistic in a society whose parts are increasingly becoming economically interdependent.

Numerous community development corporations have been organized in ghetto areas to operate manufacturing facilities and thereby provide job opportunities for residents. Their potential for success is handicapped by an inner-city location with poor industrial sites, inadequate utilities and transportation facilities, high insurance rates, and unskilled labor. Most development corporations have experienced serious difficulties in attracting the necessary capital from traditional sources. Where outside capital has been furnished, the supplying organization has severely restricted the discretion of the corporation in an effort to make the venture successful. Restrictions are placed on the purposes for which funds may be expended, and managers may be required to have certain training and experience. The intensely desired local control in most instances will have to be forfeited if major outside financing is to be attracted for the support of commercial and industrial activities. The conclusion is inescapable that community development corporations will have relatively little success in solving the economic, social, and political problems of ghetto areas.

Summary

The decade of the 1960's was a period of major economic, political, and social change in large central cities; yet few major institutional innovations were adopted to enable the cities to cope more effectively with the new conditions. The failure of central cities to solve their more pressing problems and rising expectations among the disadvantaged led to agitation for major reform in the institutions of municipal government, institutions largely based upon the tenets developed by the municipal reform movement which originated in the 1890's.

Agitation for the establishment of a system of neighborhood government may be traced in part to the federal government, which has played an important role as a promoter of citizen participation in cities since 1954. The urban renewal, antipoverty, and Model Cities programs made citizen participation a condition for the receipt of federal grants-in-aid.

Strong and growing support for a system of neighborhood government within large cities surfaced after 1965 as reformers urged the conversion of the unified municipal government into a federated system with the existing government responsible for functions that must be handled on a broad geographic base and newly created neighborhood governments responsible for all other functions.

Two major problems have to faced once a decision has been made to establish neighborhood governments. First, there is the difficult task of determining the optimum boundaries for such units. We have suggested five criteria that can be utilized in making the determination. The second problem involves finance. Where can funds be found to support neighborhood governments? Disadvantaged neighborhoods, in particular, lack the financial resources to support such governments, and it is improbable that cities and counties will fund the governments with no strings attached.

Chapter II

COMMUNITY SCHOOLS

In the preceding chapter we examined the origin of the neighbor-hood government movement, the rationale of its proponents, the sketchy model that has been developed, the difficulties encountered in attempting to delineate neighborhood boundaries, and the major problems that neighborhood governments would face. We now turn our attention to the neighborhood government movement as it relates to one functional area—schools.

The public school system in large cities has been declining in quality in recent years for a variety of reasons, including a growing fiscal crisis. Numerous central-city schools are old, dilapidated, and overcrowded, and many able teachers have been attracted to suburban school systems by higher salary scales and more modern facilities. Compounding the central-city school problem, in the view of the critics, has been the development of a status quo and inbred educational bureaucracy which has had a stifling impact upon the innovative spirit of teachers. The school system has been labeled a colossal educational failure by its harshest critics, who maintain that it is insulated from the public, and even its defenders admit the system has not been a success in educating disadvantaged children.

Today, the school system has become a center of battle between those supporting centralization and professionalism and those supporting community control. Recognizing that community involvement in school affairs can make the schools more responsive to neighborhood needs, a number of large cities administratively decentralized their school systems by creating local school districts and community school boards with advisory powers. Not surprisingly, a decentralized system of this nature does not satisfy the advocates of community control who contend that participatory democracy should be the guiding premise upon which a school system is developed, with parents, teachers, administrators, and students participating in the determination of policy. Community involvement in school affairs, goes the argument, would make the school more responsive to local needs and improve the quality of education. Citizen participation in the form of traditional parent-teachers associations is rejected as a totally inadequate form of participation that involves cooptation more than anything else.

To date, a type of community-controlled school system demanded by the new breed of reformers has been established in only two cities— New York and Detroit. A federated system was established in the former in 1970 and in the latter in 1971 by the devolution of certain political powers from the city level to the neighborhood or community level. In this chapter we will examine the politics of establishing a system of limited neighborhood control of schools in these two cities, paying particular attention to lessening black support for school integration and growing support for black separatism.

New York City

That pressures for school decentralization and greater public participation in the educational process developed in New York City is not surprising in view of the fact that it is a city of 8 million persons with over 1.1 million students, 60,000 professionals, and 897 schools, including 615 elementary schools, 149 junior and intermediate high schools, 62 academic high schools, 28 vocational high schools, and 43 special schools for handicapped or maladjusted students. Though the total population of the city has remained relatively stable, the influx of poor people with large families has made the student enrollment swell at a time when the economic base was shrinking because of the exodus of middle-class families and business firms to suburbia. In addition, the school system has undergone a vast upheaval in terms of the composition of its student body during the past quarter century.

The current student population of the New York City school system is 32 percent black and 22 percent Puerto Rican, and the charge is made that the system is insensitive to the needs of a school population with a changed socioeconomic composition. In terms of reading level, 85 percent of the students in Harlem are one year behind, and the Harlem dropout rate is exceptionally high. In ten predominantly black schools the proportion of fifth-grade students reading at or above their grade level ranges from 14 to 44 percent, while the range for fifth-grade students in predominantly white schools was 31 to 73 percent.

Demand for Community Control. Advocates of community control in New York City became dissatisfied with the twenty-five local school district boards appointed by the board of education in 1961 because they lacked power to determine educational policy and did little more than hold public hearings. In 1965, the number of districts was increased to thirty-one, but control over budgeting and personnel remained centralized. Studies indicate that the boards did not add significant inputs to the policy-making process. As a consequence, the districts were viewed as tokenism by many alienated citizens.

In the mid-1960's, partially as a result of the civil rights movement and the federal antipoverty program, many black leaders became increasingly convinced that the New York City school system should be decentralized and community involvement increased by granting the power to allocate resources to the "powerless." Not only would the quality of education be improved, according to proponents of this view, but alienation would dissipate with community involvement in a vital public program—education.

This new attitude represented a sharp break with the previous position of black leaders. As late as 1964, their statements demanded that ghetto schools either be integrated or closed, and these schools were paralyzed that year by a massive boycott in support of their demand. Shortly thereafter, many black leaders for the first time began to advocate that black principals and teachers should be given preference in ghetto schools. In 1966, when the movement for neighborhood schools started, only two principals were black.

The precipitating factor for the change in attitude appears to involve what blacks consider to be a betrayal by the board of education. In 1967, blacks opposed the construction of Intermediate School 201 on the ground that it would be a segregated school because of its location. They were assured by the board that the school would be an integrated one, but upon its opening, the school was attended almost exclusively by black and Puerto Rican children. As a consequence, community leaders began agitating for community control of the school.

Today many of the same black leaders who in 1964 denounced the neighborhood school concept for perpetuating *de facto* segregation appear to have adopted the position of white segregationists. They claim that black-controlled schools can be the most effective means by which the quality of education for black children can be drastically improved and that blacks should be able to control their schools in a manner similar to white control of suburban school systems. In a sense, they are arguing for the institutionalization of separatism, a form of segregation. A contributing factor to the demand for community control is a belief that total integration can never be achieved in New York City because of the increasing black student ·body and withdrawal of white students from the system by enrollment in private schools and family moves to suburbia.

In 1967, the state legislature responded to Mayor John V. Lindsay's requests for additional school aid by passing a law—chapter 484—requiring the mayor to submit a school decentralization plan to the 1968 legislature as a condition for the receipt of additional state aid. The mayor appointed an Advisory Panel on Decentralization of the New York City Schools and selected McGeorge Bundy, President of the Ford Foundation, to head the panel. In November 1967, the advisory panel added impetus to the movement for community control of schools by recommending that the legislature establish thirty to sixty community school districts. Each district would be governed by an eleven-member board. To assure community control, parents would elect six members; the mayor would appoint the other five in order to achieve balanced representation of all groups in each district. Each board would be authorized to determine the curriculum and use of buildings, select classroom materials, hire and fire teachers, and grant tenure. Funds would be distributed to each local board in accordance with an established formula by the city-wide board of education, which would retain control over three functions—construction of school facilities, management of the quality incentive funds to be distributed to community boards, and collective bargaining, The city board also would be empowered to monitor the performance of community boards and report its finding to the State Commissioner of Education.

The Bundy Plan for greater public participation in the school system was attacked strongly by the Council of Supervisory Associations and the 55,000-member United Federation of Teachers (UFT), a union favoring administrative decentralization. Fears were expressed that professionalism would be undermined, racial segregation would be promoted, and black teachers would espouse antiwhite sentiments in classrooms. If as many as sixty districts were created, it was charged black extremists would take over complete control of some districts and drive out white teachers and principals. Moderate black leaders have denounced black militants who wish to drive white teachers out of the school by describing such a policy as retrogression which would deprive black children of experienced teachers and block ultimate integration. Less than 10 percent of the teachers and only a few administrators currently are black. The New York Board of Rabbis criticized the plan as a "potential breeder of local apartheid" on the ground that the plan would result in distintegration and destruction of the public school system. Middle-class white citizens held divided views on the plan. Many favored administrative decentralization and professionalism over increased public participation because they believed that ghetto neighborhoods lacked the trained people and leadership necessary to make a system of community control work. Others feared a return to parochialism in the form of black nationalism and separatism.

The movement for grass-roots control of schools received major support in 1967 when the Ford Foundation decided to fund three demonstration districts—Ocean Hill-Brownsville, Intermediate School 201 Complex, and Two Bridges—in ghetto areas. Each district had approximately 9,000 students. Following their creation, the boards of the demonstration districts held that they should control their own budgets, establish the curriculum, and hire and fire teachers. The city board of education replied that it lacked legal authority to delegate these powers. There was strong opposition to the experimental districts, and the Council of Supervisory Associations went to court to block the districts by contending that professionalism was essential to prevent chaos and corruption.

The three districts—Ocean Hill-Brownsville, in particular—were centers of controversy involving parents, militants, UFT, and others as tension ebbed and flowed. Friction between UFT and ghetto parents developed when the schools in the districts remained open during the 1967 city-wide strike of teachers called by UFT.

In the Spring of 1968, the governing board of the Ocean Hill-Brownsville demonstration district attempted to oust thirteen teachers, five assistant principals, and one principal from the district without formal charges. The board's action prompted UFT to remove 350 members from the district in order to force reinstatement of the 19 who had been discharged. This dispute unfortunately fanned racial animosity since the chiefly black and Puerto Rican district was pitted against what it labeled a repressive white-power structure—UFT, many of whose members were Jewish. Anti-Semitism reared its ugly head.

The measure of success achieved by these districts prior to their absorption into larger districts in 1970 is a subject of considerable controversy. With respect to administrative personnel, six new principals were appointed by the Ocean Hill-Brownsville governing board, including the first Chinese and Puerto Rican principals to be appointed in the city. Some observers contend that the districts operated during a period of turmoil and it is impossible to measure the effect of the turmoil on the quality of education.

Although the achievement level of pupils in the three districts was below average, supporters of community control of schools claim that citizen participation increased, vandalism and teacher absences were reduced, and reading skills were improved. They add that insufficient time and funds as well as the miniscule amount of assistance provided by the board of education restricted the potential of the districts. Other district leaders and citizens feel frustrated by the experience and have become alienated, contending that it is impossible to work within an educational system hostile to minority groups.

City-wide Decentralization. During the 1968 session of the state legislature, Mayor John V. Lindsay, Governor Nelson A. Rockefeller, and the State Board of Regents supported a bill that would have granted community school boards nearly complete control over their schools. This was the most controversial issue faced by the legislature during the entire session. The turmoil in the Ocean Hill-Brownsville experimental school district confirmed the fear of conservative legislators that political decentralization of schools would be tantamount to handing control of a number of districts over to the militants.

Strong opposition from the city's board of education, UFT, the Council of Supervisory Associations, building trades and electrical workers unions, and other groups blocked passage of the bill. UFT spent an estimated $250,000 for advertisements and lobbying activities to defeat a bill that threatened its political power by authorizing the breaking up of the school system into autonomous community systems. The other unions opposed political decentralization of schools on the ground that their interests—protection for custodians, dues collections, and issuance of maintenance and construction contracts—were inadequately protected.

Following extended debate and political maneuvering, the state legislature in 1969 enacted a law—chapter 330—decentralizing New York City's school system by establishing a federated system with limited community control effective July 1, 1970. Representing a compromise between the existing system and independent community school districts, the law has been criticized for giving too much and too little power to local communities. A number of critics contend that the law provides for administrative decentralization and not community control, since local school boards do not control curricula, finances, and personnel.

An interim board of education, composed of one member appointed by each of the five borough presidents, was directed to appoint a chancellor with powers similar to those possessed by a superintendent of schools and divide the city into thirty to thirty-three districts. Each district must contain at least 20,000 students, and district lines may be readjusted in odd-numbered years.

Supporters of the three demonstration districts lost the battle to preserve the integrity of their districts. Each new district had a student population slightly less than one half the minimum number mandated by the law. The number of districts was kept at approximately thirty, as desired by UFT, to conform as nearly as possible to the existing thirty-one districts and also to make it more difficult for militants or other special interests to capture control of a district. Small districts obviously would be more susceptible to such control.

Each district is governed by a community school board composed of nine unsalaried members elected at-large for a two-year term by proportional representation, an electoral system discussed in Chapter 4. The community school boards have jurisdiction over public schools from prekindergarten through junior high school. Each board may hire and establish the salary of a district superintendent of schools, contract for repairs and maintenance up to $250,000 annually, determine the curriculum in conformance with city and state standards, recommend school sites, submit an annual budget to the chancellor, operate social centers and recreational programs, and appoint teacher aides.

The city board of education remains in charge of high schools and special schools not under the jurisdiction of community boards and is authorized to suspend, remove, or supersede a community school board or remove any of its members. In addition, the board of education retains extensive financial and personnel powers, including the preparation of the capital budget and the disciplining and licensing of teachers.

The interim board was to have been replaced on May 5, 1970, by a board composed of five members elected by the voters and two members appointed by the mayor, but the 1970 legislature extended the interim board's life for two years. Responding to the argument that an election would reopen the issue of the political decentralization of the school system, the 1972 legislature enacted a law—chapter 29—postponing the election to 1974.

The decentralization statute contains a number of ambiguities relative to the powers of community boards. For example, a community board is authorized to "appoint, define the duties, assign, promote, and discharge all its employees and fix their compensation and terms of employment." Yet the city board of education "for all purposes" is declared to "be the government or public employer of all persons appointed or assigned by the city board or the community boards." These ambiguities may be resolved by time, legislation, or court decisions.

Insufficient time has passed to allow other than a very preliminary assessment of the community school system in New York City. *The New York Times* surveyed the city's schools at the end of the first year of decentralized operations, and reported that "school officials and organizations . . . said that the reform move had sparked increased public interest and involvement in school matters."[1] District board meetings often attracted hundreds of citizens, and many presented their views on the items on the agenda. These meetings are in sharp contrast to the meetings held by the old appointed community school boards which possessed only advisory powers; their meetings attracted only a handful of citizens. According to the survey, there also has been "a heightened degree of responsiveness to community needs on the part of local school authorities."

Detroit

Detroit, along with a number of other cities, had administratively decentralized its school system by 1969. Detroit's school system had become the fifth largest system in the country and was experiencing serious problems in financing its schools. The city had nine school districts, each headed by a deputy superintendent of schools, when the state legislature in that year enacted a limited political decentralization law —Public Act 244. The law mandated the establishment by January 30, 1970, of seven to eleven school districts within the 295,000 pupil Detroit school system, only 37 percent of whom are white. Each district was required to have 25,000 to 50,000 students.

The decentralization act was not endorsed by the Detroit Board of Education or by blacks favoring a proposal for community control of schools. Blacks account for 63 percent of the total Detroit school enrollment and 42 percent of the teachers. The powerful Detroit Federation of Teachers was able to have written into the law guarantees of the federation's bargaining, seniority, and tenure rights as well as other benefits.

Development of the Plan. Public hearings were conducted by the Detroit Board of Education during the fall of 1969, and seven alternative plans were released to the public on March 30, 1970. An explanatory statement pointed out that the board was legally required to adopt a plan providing for racially integrated districts and adhering to the one-man, one-vote requirement established by the United States Supreme Court. Each plan reflected the board's fear that decentralization would foster segregation and its desire to maximize integration, thereby minimizing the possibility of black control of several districts. The board's alternative plans prompted the West Central Organization to develop its own alternative plan, labeled the Black Plan, which received the support of Parents and Students for Community Schools, a coalition of black community organizations. The board gave little consideration to this plan in reaching a final determination.

The April 7, 1970, board meeting at which action was to be taken was a volatile one attended by hundreds of white parents opposed to integration. At the stormy meeting, the board by a four-to-two vote adopted a plan providing for seven districts and changing the feeder pattern of twelve of the twenty-two high schools. In an effort to preserve school integration, approximately 3,000 entering high school students would be transferred from neighborhood schools to others located miles away in racially disturbed inner-city neighborhoods.

The officially approved plan precipitated boycotts at several predominantly white schools located on the fringes of the city, produced threats of lawsuits and citizen resistance, and led to predictions that the exodus of white families from the city would be spurred. Under the plan, white enrollment at Denby and Redford High Schools—which are located near the outskirts of the city—would drop from 97 percent to 54 percent and 29 percent respectively in 1972.

White opponents of the plan organized the Citizens Committee for Better Education and collected 130,000 signatures on petitions to recall the four board members who voted in favor of the decentralization plan. On August 4, 1970, the four were recalled. Subsequently, Governor William G. Milliken appointed replacements to serve until December 31, 1970.

The 1970 Act. Following considerable debate, the 1970 legislature enacted a new law—Public Act 48—repealing the 1969 law. The new law required the establishment of eight regional school districts by January 1, 1971, and provided for an open system in which pupils would be allowed to transfer from racially integrated schools. (Under the previous policy, a student could transfer schools only if such action promoted integration.) The new law also forbade district boundary changes.

The new act was approved unanimously in the state senate; in the legislature it was supported by an unusual political coalition—

conservative white, liberal white, and black legislators. White conservatives were opposed to integration, white liberals feared racial confrontation if the old law was not repealed, and blacks wished to trade integration for community control. Mayor Roman Gribbs warned the governor that racial disorders might occur if the boundary changes in the original act were not overturned.

Under provisions of the 1970 law, the governor was authorized to appoint a three-member Detroit Boundary Commission charged with responsibility for establishing school regions for electoral purposes. Each region is governed by a five-member board elected on November 3, 1970. The member receiving the most votes serves as chairman of the board and as an ex officio member of the central board. The latter was converted from a seven-member to a thirteen-member body—five members elected at-large and the chairman of each of the eight regional boards. Even though the majority of the population in six regions is black, blacks won only three seats on the thirteen-member central board (three of the old seven-member board of education were black) and a majority of the seats on only two regional boards.

Each regional board is authorized to employ a superintendent of schools from a list of candidates submitted by the central board; discharge the superintendent; "employ and discharge, assign, and promote all teachers and other employees" subject to review by the central board; determine the curriculum and use of school facilities; establish educational and testing programs; and determine the budget for the region based upon funds allocated by the central board. The central board retains responsibility for allocation of capital funds, bonding, central purchasing, contract negotiations, payrolls, property management and maintenance, special education programs, and preparation of guidelines for the regional boards. Lacking funds to implement the act, the board of education applied for and received a $360,000 grant from the Ford Foundation.

The 1970 act was challenged in the courts by the National Association for the Advancement of Colored People (NAACP) on the ground that it would not promote racial balance in the faculty and student body in each school. The Sixth Circuit Court of Appeals, on October 13, ruled a section of the act unconstitutional, and the Federal District Court, on November 4, directed the Detroit Board of Education to present to the court by November 16th a plan that would achieve at least the same degree of racial integration as the April 7 plan.

On December 3, 1970, District Court Judge Stephen Roth declared that "integration for integration's sake alone is self-defeating" and rejected forced busing. Instead, he ordered the adoption of a plan providing for the establishment of "magnet" high schools. Each school would be specialized—arts, business, science, vocational—and students would be allowed to select their programs and schools, effective in the fall of 1971. The plan was proposed by board of education member Patrick McDonald who believed that quality, specialized high schools would attract an integrated student body.

Conclusions cannot be drawn relative to the effectiveness of the regional school boards for two reasons. First, the boards have been in existence only since January 1, 1971. Second, the boards have been operating during a period of acute financial problems.

The Detroit school district has not operated in accordance with sound financial practices for a number of years. On several occasions the board of education has adopted deficit budgets contrary to state law and since 1968 has failed to adopt a budget prior to the start of the fiscal year. The budget for 1969-1970 was adopted seven months after the start of the fiscal year, and the budget for fiscal 1971-1972 was adopted two and one half months late.

Public Act 48 stipulates that each regional school board has authority to "determine the budget for the region and the schools therein based upon the allocation of funds received from" the city board of education. The late adoption of the budget for the first year of the decentralized school system has caused a major problem since personnel had been hired and schools reopened prior to the adoption of the budget. As a consequence, the total proposed expenditures of the eight regional boards, submitted to the central board in November and December, exceeded the level of allocation by more than $5 million.

Summary

That many large-city school systems have failed to provide a good education for numerous disadvantaged children cannot be denied. A significant percentage of these children read below their grade level, and their dropout rate is excessively high. Not surprisingly, leaders of disadvantaged communities have played a major role in the establishment of a politically decentralized school system in New York City and Detroit.

For a variety of reasons, a significant number of black leaders in New York City in the mid-1960's began to abandon their support of school integration as the best strategy for the improvement of the quality of education for black children. These leaders worked for the establishment of a system of community-controlled schools. Black leaders in Detroit supported the establishment of a community school system for basically the same reasons. It is significant that both community school systems were established by a mandate of the state legislature.

As we saw in Chapter 1, no genuine multifunctional neighborhood government has been created in any city. The establishment of limited community control of schools in New York City and Detroit makes it appear reasonable that this is the only form of neighborhood government that will be adopted in the immediate future.

Chapter III

ADMINISTRATIVE RESPONSE

We have seen in the preceding chapters that urban problems are of great magnitude and complexity, alienation is endemic in many neighborhoods, and demands for neighborhood government appear to be growing. City officials are fully aware of the seriousness of the problems they must cope with daily, but many do not fully appreciate the stronghold that alienation has gained.

The mayor, at the apex of the administrative pyramid, is besieged by demands from municipal employees and their unions as well as from neighborhoods. Even a mayor with strong formal powers finds that in a large city he often is unable to move the bureaucracy sufficiently to improve the delivery of services in response to neighborhood requests with which he is in full sympathy. "Politicosclerosis," or hardening of the arteries of political communications, results from the gap between citizens and what appears to be an unfathomable government. The proliferation of municipal offices, since 1945, some with overlapping responsibilities, has perplexed many citizens. Information is difficult to obtain, and the registration of complaints is hindered by the inaccessibility of the responsible officials.

Some critics maintain that overcentralization of authority in city hall is responsible at least partially for the lack of program variations to meet unique conditions in individual neighborhoods. Bureaucratization and professionalization are identified as the culprits responsible for an unresponsive government. The large bureaucracy, headed by professionals, tends to decide what is best for the city and often appears to be relatively independent of control by elected officials. Defenders of bureaucracy attribute the lack of responsiveness to a lack of resources.

Since the mid-1960's mayors have revealed a willingness to experiment with new institutional arrangements designed to increase popular participation in neighborhood and municipal affairs. Their administrations have responded in two principal ways to the charges of their indifference and unresponsiveness to the needs of citizens, particularly those heavily dependent upon governmental services. First, attempts have been made to establish and improve communications between neighborhoods and city hall by means of a continuing dialogue. It is hoped that the dialogue will allow residents to sensitize local administrators to neighborhood needs and aspirations and enable administrators to anticipate problems. Second, attempts have been made to improve the delivery of services by providing them on a decentralized basis, thereby reducing the area within which decisions are made and improving administrative coordination. While city hall has been pushing administrative decentralization of services to allow neighborhood variations, it opposes political decentralization in the form of neighborhood control of institutions and services as advocated by the new reformers.

The administrative response of city hall to growing complaints about inadequate delivery of services and demands for neighborhood government has been a piecemeal one. The innovations, designed to reduce stress in the system, generally have been launched as experiments on an *ad hoc* basis rather than within the framework of an overall plan to make the city government more responsive to neighborhood needs and desires. Not surprisingly, mayors have experienced opposition to some of their administrative innovations from public employee unions, which have been growing in power.

We can place cities in four categories relative to their administrative response to neighborhood pressures. In the first category are cities that have made no visible response to these pressures. Cities in the second category have limited their response to new mechanisms to facilitate neighborhood-city hall communications. The third category includes cities that have placed increased reliance upon administrative decentralization to deliver services more effectively on the neighborhood level. In the fourth category are cities, such as New York City, that have launched both new communications and decentralization programs.

Improved Communications

The complexity and geographical scale of a sprawling large city with its labyrinthine network of relationships between departments and agencies contributes to the belief that the city government is inaccessible and unresponsive. New York City, for example, has a population larger than that of sixty-six member nations of the United Nations. It also has a massive bureaucracy with approximately 260,000 employees and a police department of 37,500—larger than the army of most nations. And Los Angeles covers an area of 455 square miles or twice the area of Chicago.

Complaint Systems. The popularity of "Action Line" columns in numerous local newspapers across the United States clearly demonstrates that citizens believe they need a central source of information and a place where they can register complaints. Furthermore, in twenty-two different cities, the Urban Coalition—a nonprofit corporation seeking to create a new economic, moral, political, and social climate—sponsors and subsidizes in part a popular "Call for Action" radio program; volunteers answer the telephones and follow up citizen complaints with city departments.

The inability of residents in many cities to effectively register complaints and obtain information has accentuated their feelings of powerlessness. In particular, citizens registering complaints resent being shuffled from one department to another with the excuse that the other department has jurisdiction over a particular type of complaint. To many citizens, it may appear that the city is attempting to discourage the filing of complaints. It should not be necessary for a citizen to contact a councilman about inadequate administrative performance, but often a citizen has no other alternative if he wishes to register a complaint.

Recognizing that the procedure for the redress of grievances is inadequate, 136 local governments of over 25,000 population have established and publicized a special complaint telephone number as an access mechanism to help citizens penetrate the complex bureaucracy. Closely associated with the installation of a complaint telephone number has been the creation in 161 cities of over 25,000 population of a complaint bureau staffed by a "grievance man" whose function is the redress of grievances and elimination of injustices.

San Diego in 1967 created the position of "Citizens Assistance Officer," a special assistant to the city manager, who not only receives complaints from citizens but also processes all written communications from councilmen to the manager. Common complaints involve neighbors, pets, and automobiles. Most of the one hundred weekly complaints handled by the volunteer workers of the information and complaint agency in Wilmington, Delaware, are directed against inadequate city services—garbage collection and snow removal most commonly.

In Georgia, Savannah in November 1968 appointed a "Community Services Officer," and DeKalb County in 1969 created a service desk designed to handle citizen complaints not remedied by a department or incapable of being channeled to a department. In practice, however, citizens file complaints with the service desk without first attempting to contact a department, and complaints about the court and school systems are received although the Board of County Commissioners has no jurisdiction over these two systems.

In Indianapolis, Houston, Los Angeles, Jacksonville, and New York, the complaint bureau is located in the mayor's office. In New York City, Volunteers for Good Government answer the telephones in the Mayor's Information Office from 5 p.m. to midnight seven nights a week. The position of "Night Mayor," established by Mayor John V. Lindsay in 1966, and manned by high-level officials, is somewhat comparable to the military "Officer of the Day." Serving from 6:30 p.m. until dawn, the "Night Mayor" not only provides information and initiates needed action but also commonly makes a field inspection.

Charlotte, North Carolina, in 1969 created a Public Service and Information Department and placed it in charge of the "Citizen Action Line" or "Hot Line." In the 80,000 water bills mailed each month, the department inserts an "Action Report" providing information on municipal activities not normally covered in the local newspapers.

Stockton, California, experimented with "Neighbormen" who were to perform a liaison function between city hall and neighborhoods, especially disadvantaged ones. The "Neighbormen" were involved in handling many citizen complaints, but the program was abandoned by the city council in 1969.

Complaint bureaus can be of service by soliciting suggestions for improving municipal services and relieving departments of many requests for basic information or information on matters not under their jurisdiction. The complaint telephone number undoubtedly has some value as a therapeutic device, since it allows citizens to let off steam even though the city may not be in a position to initiate corrective action. The fact that the citizen can call city hall and register a complaint may in some small way satisfy an irate John Q. Public. The function of a special telephone number or bureau is not simply to receive complaints and relay them to the appropriate departments for action, however. A function of at least equal importance is answering questions and in some cases informing citizens that the complaints are groundless or should be directed to a county, state, or federal office.

Analysis of complaints to discover patterns can assist administrators in keeping attuned to the changing needs in various parts of the city and may serve as one method of evaluating the performance of various departments and highlighting the need for administrative changes. To date, however, there is no evidence that adequate records of complaints are being kept and analyzed. In a study of complaint-handling arrangements in nine areas, Paul Dolan of the University of Delaware found that records either were not kept or were inadequate.[1] An Institute of Local Self Government study of the handling of grievances in seventeen California cities over 100,000 population and the twenty largest counties revealed that records of grievances generally are not kept by the city manager or chief administrative officer in three fourths of the cities.[2] The study adds:

> The complaint window found in some city halls is perhaps more suited to handle holes in the street or infrequency of garbage collection. It is doubtful if it is appropriate to the nature of many current citizen grievances in urban areas. One doesn't get very far at a complaint window espousing community development ordinances. No human relations commission was ever organized at a complaint window; no institutions for increased involvement of citizens in local government processes were ever devised there.[3]

The installation of a complaint telephone number or bureau is opposed by a number of local officials on the ground that it will generate complaints. This, of course, is one of its purposes. In addition, some administrators maintain that they perform a type of "ombudsman" function without the label. It must be questioned, however, whether a busy, high-level administrator, such as a city manager or mayor, can devote the time necessary to keeping in close contact with the needs and wishes of citizens in general and minority citizens in particular. The disadvantaged generally do not know the procedure for registering complaints and are reluctant to contact such an exalted official as the city manager or mayor. Furthermore, an administrator cannot perform the true ombudsman's function of independent criticism of the city administration.

Although there has been considerable discussion relative to the creation by cities of the position of ombudsman, or "humanizer," no city has established a true one of the Scandinavian variety: a high-level, impartial official—appointed by the city council and independent of the mayor or city manager—responsible for protecting citizens' rights and liberties against bureaucratic abuse.

Only two local governments currently have ombudsmen. The Home

Rule charter for King County, Washington, mandated the establishment of an Office of Citizens Complaints with authority to investigate complaints by subpoenaing witnesses and making and publicizing recommendations relative to its findings. During 1970, the office received 1,994 complaints, involving 707 separate cases. Of the total, 699 cases have been closed, 8 are pending, and 206 were transferred to other agencies since they fell outside the jurisdiction of the office. Experience in King County indicates that the number of complaints is related to weather conditions and holidays. The largest number of complaints is received on rainy Mondays; few complaints are received on a sunny Friday afternoon. The number of complaints also decreases sharply immediately prior to and during holiday periods; Christmas Eve was the first day during which not one complaint was registered.

In 1971, Seattle and King County established the Joint Seattle-King County Office of the Ombudsman and Citizen Complaints. The Montgomery County (Virginia) School Board in 1970 created the Office of Ombudsman to investigate complaints independent of the school administration. The school system had a so-called "ombudsman" for the two previous years, but he reported to the deputy superintendent of schools. An ombudsman generally acts upon the receipt of complaints, but he can investigate on his own initiative. Being outside the bureaucratic chain of command, he cannot reverse an administrative decision; his corrective weapons are persuasion, publicity, and reports to the council. He often functions as a mediator, a protector of administrators against unfounded charges, and a commentator on the need for changes in laws.

Mayors, as one would imagine, have not been enthusiastic about the creation of the position of ombudsman and prefer the appointment of an official under their personal control to handle complaints. Yet popular support for complaint officers appointed by the mayor tends to be lacking, since the public often views them as part of the "establishment" whose function is to protect it rather than to serve as an independent investigatory body.

City councilmen historically have performed a limited ombudsman function. Provided they had the time and staff, they could serve as true ombudsmen; but there is the danger that they might interfere in routine administration and create a situation that existed in the past in many weak mayor cities where department heads did not know whether they were responsible to the mayor or to a councilman or council committee. Consequently, one must conclude that councilmanic handling of complaints and grievances is an inadequate substitute for an ombudsman.

In his study of complaint-handling arrangements, Paul Dolan discovered that councilmen commonly opposed an ombudsman office.

> The complaint officer was looked upon by the majority of the councilmen as an interloper in the executive-legistlative relationship. He was suspected of serving as the mayor's aide in securing public services or doing favors under the guise of expediting services, thus undermining the councilman's position with his constituents.[4]

Dolan reports that councilmen want to act as ombudsmen in their own districts and therefore do not appropriate sufficient funds to enable the complaint agencies to carry on adequate programs. Councilmen generally take the position that numerous elected officials handle grievances on a daily basis and that an ombusdman would undermine the position of administrators. Furthermore, councilmen believe that an ombudsman would relieve them of their grievance rectification function and the votes that it wins.

Police-Community Relations Units. The problem of community relations first became apparent to the police department in its dealings with ghetto neighborhoods. Residents of such areas have frequent and abrasive contact with the police, who are expected to cope with the massive social chaos and change associated with poverty. Many ghetto residents are recent migrants from rural areas and are unaccustomed to life in the city. The situation is further complicated by small groups of black militants who provoke trouble with the police in order to spark civil disorders. A special Gallup public opinion survey made for *Newsweek* in 1971 revealed that "nearly two-thirds of all whites are deeply skeptical about charges of police brutality, but more than half the blacks believe that such charges are at least fairly likely to be true."[5]

The police, it is contended, harass local residents, especially young adult males, and often overreact to a minor disturbance, thereby touching off a much more major disturbance. There can be no denying that the precipitating incident for disorders usually has involved the police, and the President's Commission on Law Enforcement and Administration of Justice proposed that a citizen advisory committee be created in each police precinct.

Numerous police departments have created complaint review boards to investigate charges of police brutality, use of excessive force, discourtesy, and discrimination. A major debate has centered around the question of whether the review board should be independent of the police department. New York City's Police Department, for example, has a review board composed of five civilian employees of the department. This arrangement, however, does not satisfy critics who demand a completely independent civilian review board. J. Edgar Hoover maintained that the effectiveness of a police force in controlling civil disorders is weakened by a review board independent of the department. He added, with respect to the 1964 summer riots, that "where there is an outside review board the restraint of the police was so great that effective action against the rioters appeared impossible."[6]

As of 1970, 44 percent of 650 cities surveyed by the International City Management Association (ICMA) have activated special police-community relations units to foster mutual understanding, thereby reducing friction. The programs are located primarily in large cities. In a similar study conducted one year earlier, 475 out of 654 cities reported to the ICMA that they offer training programs in police-community relations.

In St. Louis, Missouri, each police district has a committee composed of residents and policemen; subcommittees deal with automobile theft, juvenile delinquency, public relations, sanitation problems, traffic congestion, and stimulation of voluntary action by residents. The Winston-Salem police-community relations unit, launched in 1966 and initially privately financed, performs a liaison function between the deprived and sources of aid and has an office in the Model Cities area. Policemen are given an intensive training program; the curriculum was prepared by the Institute of Government of the University of North Carolina and the Urban Affairs Institute of Wake Forest University. Inaugurated in October 1967, Houston's police-community relations program is designed to bring each member of the 1500-man force together with residents of minority communities for small-group discussions of municipal problems. The effectiveness of the program is reflected in a sharp decline in the number of complaints directed against the police received by the National Association for the Advancement of Colored People and the mayor's office.

The Human Relations Section of the Dallas Police Department, set up following a 1968 reorganization, operates store front community service centers, staffed by volunteer policemen, in four low-income neighborhoods that have a high crime rate. The staff of each center attends community meetings in order to discover major problems and complaints and to promote public support for law enforcement. The most frequent complaints involve junk automobiles, inadequate street lighting, poor condition of street pavement and signs, and weeds in vacant lots; complaints that fall outside the jurisdiction of the police department are referred to the appropriate agency. The centers also receive requests for additional patrols and provide assistance in obtaining drivers' licenses and completing injury reports. They distribute donated food to needy families, provide transportation to area hospitals, assist residents to find employment and obtain welfare services, and have organized a baseball league for boys. Citizen reaction has been favorable although many citizens have misinterpreted the function of the centers and view them as police precincts whose function is law enforcement.

San Diego has four "store-front" offices operated by the Police Department's Community Relations Division. In 1969, the department began another experiment by inviting young persons to ride in police cruisers on trouble calls and watch the police in action. Following their tour, the young people discuss the experience with the policemen and the next day hold discussions with the police chief. Reaction to the "Ride-Along" program has been very favorable, and youngsters sign up two months in advance.

There is little evidence to date that police-community relations units have encouraged citizens to report crimes or significantly reduced friction between the police and the black community. In the minds of many ghetto residents, the units appear to be little more than public relations mechanisms.

In an effort to improve police-community relations in black ghettos, most large cities in the mid-1960's launched a program to recruit additional black policemen. The replacement of white policemen by black ones in black areas, it was felt, would lessen popular acceptance of the concept that policemen are members of an occupying colonial army. Recruitment of blacks is hindered, however, by discrimination against blacks in many departments, the negative image of the police held by young blacks, and the failure of a large number of blacks to pass written civil service examinations.

To date only the District of Columbia has succeeded in adding a significant number of blacks to its police force; other cities have added only a few blacks, and the percentage of blacks on the force has remained substantially unchanged and even declined in a few cities. New York City, to cite only one example, increased the number of blacks on its police force from 5.0 percent to 7.5 percent between 1960 and 1970. Boston is the only major city which has established an all-black police unit to operate in a black ghetto neighborhood. In November 1971, the Boston police commissioner created a thirty-four member black strike force, commanded by a black deputy superintendent, to patrol the Roxbury section of the city.

Little City Halls. The establishment of neighborhood city halls or municipal service centers, recommended by the National Advisory Commission on Civil Disorders, represents a major organizational attempt to make city officials more available to citizens. The halls are designed to strengthen lines of communications between citizens and their government and to provide feedback to city hall, thereby allowing the city to anticipate problems and initiate corrective action where needed. In a number of cities, the "little" city halls are information and complaint referral agencies only; in other cities, the halls also provide such services as issuing licenses and accepting tax payments. Many neighborhood city halls are financed by grants from the Office of Economic Opportunity, Safe Streets Act of 1968, and the Model Cities program.

The little city halls are clearly part of a deliberate strategy to convince citizens, especially in poverty areas, that their government cares about their needs and is not remote and unresponsive. The halls, however, have been criticized on the ground that they raise neighborhood expectations and then lack the power to deliver. Only six cities report that their "mini" city halls have advisory boards composed of neighborhood residents; this is a surprisingly small number in view of the fact that the halls are intended to maximize communications.

There is no agreement as to the population size that should be served by a little city hall. The National Commission on Urban Problems in 1968 suggested a population of 25,000 to 50,000 and added that there may be no need to have halls throughout an entire city.[7] The Commission suggested that "decentralized services—police, public welfare, and the like—should be encouraged to hire local residents."[8]

Little city halls originated in Los Angeles, where the first ones were opened in the 1920's as areas were annexed to the city. In 1950, the Los Angeles Planning Commission adopted a city-wide Branch Administrative Center Plan providing for a system of administrative or civic centers throughout the 455 square miles of the city. Twelve centers—staffed by officials of city, county, state, and federal agencies— are currently in operation. Each center provides administrative services, and many offer cultural, recreational, and social services in addition. The centers not only maximize public access and convenience but also facilitate interagency and interjurisdictional coordination.

In 1960, San Antonio opened the first of its three neighborhood service centers, each serving a population of approximately 200,000. One center is staffed by a supervisor, twenty-five inspectors, and twenty-five other employees. Not only does the center bring the government physically close to the people, but it also allows building and health inspectors to familiarize themselves thoroughly with one area of the city. Automotive shops and equipment facilities are located in each area, thereby enabling quicker service in response to requests. The three cen-

ters employ in excess of nine hundred employees and have budgets totaling more than $7 million annually.

Hartford, Connecticut, in 1963 organized the first of its three field
teams whose goal is the improved delivery of services.[9] A representative from the city manager's office was made field coordinator of a
team composed of housing inspectors and welfare, police, and sanitation employees in a sixteen-block area. Joining the team were two job
counselors from the state labor department, a representative of the state
civil rights commission, and members of the Visiting Nurse Association.

Kansas City, Missouri, has two "City Hall Annexes," opened in
1965 and 1968, which accept payments for taxes, water bills, and certain licenses in addition to serving as information centers. The two
annexes currently process approximately 30,000 transactions annually.

In 1969, Santa Fe Springs, California, opened a Neighborhood
Center for Social Services in a sixty-five acre section of the city popu-
lated by Mexican-Americans. The center's director reports to the city
manager, and its ten-member advisory committee is composed of five
residents and five representatives of private and public agencies utilizing the center. Programs include legal services, job placement, physical
and mental health care, senior citizen activities, and counseling.

In New York City councilmen have opposed Mayor John V.
Lindsay's plan for developing neighborhood city halls on the ground
they would become part of the mayor's political machine, and in 1966,
the council deleted a $200,000 appropriation item for thirty-two halls.
Majority leader David Ross charged "that the Mayor was proposing
nothing more than a string of political clubhouses for himself. He is
saying, in effect, these local storefronts did very well for me during the
campaign, let's keep them open for another four years until the next
campaign."[10] In January 1967, Mayor Lindsay sought to mollify council
opposition by proposing that each councilman be given office space in
each hall in his district and control of one half of the jobs in each hall.
Citizens Union, a good government association, has also opposed the
halls on the ground they remove a duty from community planning
boards whose jurisdictions generally coincide with "historic communities." Five privately financed "mini" city halls, however, have
been operating as information and complaint-handling centers with a
staff of as many as six individuals. The director of each hall calls a
periodic meeting at which the directors of the decentralized operations of
city agencies can learn first hand the complaints of citizens and discuss
ways to improve interagency coordination.

In 1968 Mayor Lindsay created forty-eight urban action task forces,
each composed of neighborhood civic leaders and heads of munic-

ipal units providing services. The task forces were established in order to obtain information on discontent which might erupt into civil disorder, but they have been turned into informal devices for the performance of functions normally performed by little city halls. The task forces regularly operate in less than one half of the city's sixty-two community districts. Under the chairmanship of a member of the mayor's cabinet, a task force periodically meets in a neighborhood to discuss problems and methods for improving the delivery of services and to receive and transmit complaints to the proper city agency. The nature of citizen participation changes continually since the citizen membership is based upon self-selection. Forty neighborhoods have a local task force office that is usually staffed by two residents of the neighborhood. Each task force submits weekly reports to the mayor's office on neighborhood problems, such as crime and garbage collection, in order to allow remedial action to be instituted to avert potential crises. If a civil disorder threatens to occur in a given neighborhood, the task force calls upon local leaders to "cool" the situation. Faced with a serious budget crisis, Mayor Lindsay ordered the closing of the neighborhood task force offices effective May 1, 1971, but fourteen of the offices were reopened that same month after community groups raised the needed funds.

Boston opened the first of its little city halls in July 1968 and currently has fifteen. Seven have bilingual staffs, including a notary public, a fire inspector, a social security representative, and one to three senior aides who work with the elderly. Staff members register voters, file applications for tax abatement and public housing, accept payments for various tax bills, and help citizens obtain copies of official records such as birth and marriage certificates. Over 80,000 complaints are filed at the halls annually. The managers of Boston little city halls do not simply sit in the halls and wait for residents to come to them; it is their responsibility to attend neighborhood meetings and seek out residents with problems. Although it was originally felt that the manager would be more effective if he lived in the neighborhood, it was finally decided that he should not live in the area in order to emphasize that he is not a political rival of the neighborhood politicians. Most staff members, however, are residents of the neighborhoods in which their halls are located. The halls have been accepted by the politicians, who refer constituents to the halls, and the sharp increase in the number of citizens walking into the halls appears to indicate a growing public acceptance of their ability to be of service.

Richmond, Virginia, in April 1968 created five neighborhood service teams, composed of officials of nine departments, to function as little city halls in poverty areas and improve city hall-neighborhood communications. Although the initial reaction to the teams was good, attendance at the weekly meetings dwindled during the first half of 1969, and it was decided to revamp the program. The five teams have been replaced by an official from each of four departments—public health, public safety, public works, and recreation and parks—who devotes half of his time to the little city hall program getting to know his neighborhood, meeting with neighborhood organizations, and accepting requests for city services.

In several cities—for example, Los Angeles, Miami, Newburgh, New York, and Prairie, Texas—trailers or buses are used as mobile city halls. The trailer used as the mayor's mobile team in New York City is manned by communication specialists, including a Spanish-speaking team, who listen to complaints and prod city departments to initiate remedial action. Warren, Michigan, uses a camper—equipped with a two-way radio—as a mobile city hall or "action line on wheels." It has a sign stating "If I can be of service, flag me down."

Special Neighborhood Meetings. In various communities city hall has attempted to improve communications not only by establishing new channels but also by attempting to make officials more available to citizens. "Good government" associations in medium and large cities have long recognized the need for neighborhood-city hall communication. The Citizens Plan E Association of Worcester, Massachusetts, for example, has held "Little Town Meetings" in various neighborhoods on a regular basis since 1950; each "Little Town Meeting" is attended by the city manager, major department heads, one city councilor, and one school committee member.

In May 1966, Mayor Louie Welch of Houston began visiting minority neighborhoods for the purpose of holding "Meet Your Mayor" sessions. Cleveland holds "Town Hall Meetings" throughout the city at which the mayor speaks briefly, followed by a question and answer session. Mayor Harry G. Haskell, Jr., of Wilmington, Delaware, in 1969 divided the city into seven ethnic and geographic areas; meetings, attended by municipal officials and financed by private donations, are held in each area at regular intervals. The Norfolk (Virginia) Citizens Advisory Committee has worked primarily in the field of race relations, but in 1970 it instituted a series of "Townhall Meetings," at the suggestion of the mayor, to seek ideas and complaints. In May 1969, the mayor of El Paso established a Council for Social Action to promote citizen involvement in municipal affairs. Six area councils have been organized as committees under the city council to improve communication with city hall. Monthly evening meetings of the city council are scheduled in various areas on a rotating basis, with the area council arranging the meeting, preparing the agenda, and promoting citizen attendance.

In Arizona the Phoenix city council has held neighborhood meetings—called "Meetings-on-Wheels"—since 1966. These meetings became necessary as the city's population increased 500 percent from 1950 to 1970 and its area expanded from 17 to 247 square miles. The Chandler city council in March 1969 began to hold meetings in various neighborhoods, but Scottsdale's city council abandoned its policy of holding meetings in each elementary school on the ground they were not successful.

Neighborhood Councils. Popularly elected neighborhood councils, as suggested by the Committee for Economic Development in 1966 and Royal Commission on Local Government in England in 1969, are being experimented with as devices for opening and formalizing channels of communications between residents and city officials and enlisting the talents of residents in a year-round study of neighborhood problems. According to a 1971 survey conducted by Carl W. Stenberg, 140 cities with over 25,000 population have established neighborhood, area, or district councils representing residents.[11] The councils are notified that the city government plans to make decisions affecting their neighborhoods and are afforded the opportunity to confer with city officials and solicit the views of residents. When necessary, the councils mobilize as well as express neighborhood opinion. The suggestion has been advanced but not implemented that a council should be granted the power to declare *persona non grata* city officials with responsibilities in the neighborhood.

In New York City, the City Planning Commission on March 1, 1968, delineated the boundaries of sixty-two community planning districts and simultaneously established an Office of Local Area Planning to provide community planning boards with technical assistance. In defining the districts, the Commission adopted the criterion that no district should have more than 300,000 residents.

On June 16, 1969, Mayor John V. Lindsay signed Local Law 39 amending the New York City Charter by enlarging and strengthening the already existing community planning boards (or "community planning councils") and changing their name to "community boards." Each board is authorized to develop plans for its district's welfare, advise any public agency about area needs, consult with city officials, and hold public hearings. All city agencies required to hold public hearings must refer matters to the appropriate community board. A maximum of fifty members may serve on the board, borough presidents are required to consult district councilmen about appointments, and the individuals appointed must have "significant contacts with the community district." The latter provision is designed to permit nonresident businessmen and officials of institutions to serve on the boards.

To date, it appears that the borough presidents have not appointed widely representative boards but have relied heavily upon individuals active in the president's political party. Higher income groups and whites also tend to be overrepresented. In general, the larger boards have not functioned well because their size has tended to discourage attendance and participation and has increased the burden carried by the chairman.

In contrast to the Urban Action Task Forces, where participation is voluntary and self-selecting, the boards are structured in terms of citizen participation. The boards also are more concerned with long-range problems while the task forces concentrate on immediate problems. The boards, for example, assist the City Planning Commission in its periodic revision of local development plans by providing annual statements on local goals, problems, opportunities, and priorities.

The boards have generally had little visibility. Few hold more than one meeting per month, and few have continuing projects. Instead of initiating projects and requests, the boards tend to react to proposals made by city and state agencies. City agencies, however, often do not notify the boards of contemplated actions and seldom solicit their views or explain why certain actions are being taken. The boards have made few attempts to mobilize public support for their actions by holding public hearings or circulating petitions, and they seldom have tried to develop a united front with contiguous boards or to monitor the quality of services provided by city agencies. Without the expressed support of their communities and with no staff, the boards have been relatively ineffectual.

The community boards have not been totally ineffective, however. When the City Planning Commission announced on December 28, 1970, that a proposal to permit high-rise housing on north-south avenues on Manhattan's east side to exceed existing limits was being tabled, community boards 6, 7, and 8 led the fight against the proposal by attacking it as a "backdoor device" to break down the zoning law. Board 8 also claims credit for getting 50 percent of the police details off consulate duty and back on regular duties, allowing buses to operate during street closings, and blocking the Metropolitan Transportation Authority from putting a new subway tunnel under Central Park. The sharp increase in applications for seats on many boards in the early 1970's appears to reflect a growing belief that the boards are effective in protecting the interests and representing the views of their neighborhoods.

Six New York City neighborhoods also currently participate in the

Neighborhood Stabilization Plan under which up to $500,000 of capital budget funds are appropriated to a neighborhood and residents are allowed to determine how the funds should be spent to improve facilities such as parks, recreational facilities, and street lighting. To cite only one example, citizens in East Flatbush, an area with a population of 110,000, formed a twenty-nine member council and decided to utilize part of its $500,000 for visible improvements that could be made quickly—expanded library services, upgraded street lights, and two closed-circuit television systems in local schools.

Turning our attention to California, the San Mateo County Board of Supervisors in 1967 created the popularly elected East Palo Alto Municipal Council in an unincorporated area inhabited by blacks.[12] The council represents citizens before the Board of Supervisors and appoints representatives to public and private committees. Each county department solicits the council's recommendation on all matters affecting the area prior to presenting proposals to the Board of Supervisors. In nearly every case, the board has accepted the council's recommendation. Bellevue, Washington, created a community council in March 1969 when the city annexed an area of 10,000 citizens and a second council in November 1969 when 18,000 additional citizens were annexed. Each council was created for a period of four years, and its life can be extended for additional four-year periods with voter approval. A council can temporarily delay action by the city council on land use matters.[13]

Boston has organized three local advisory councils with authority to comment on plans prepared by the city, develop priorities for major improvement projects, arbitrate neighborhood disputes, and evaluate the provision of municipal services. The Boston Home Rule Commission in 1971 recommended the establishment of twelve to sixteen "little city councils." Each popularly elected council would articulate the policies and preferences of the district, have a professional staff, and evaluate the delivery of services.

In June 1970 the city council of Dayton, Ohio, acting upon the recommendation of the city manager, approved a $200,000 neighborhood grant program allowing residents to determine how the funds would be expended. The funds were allotted on a per capita basis to six areas covering the entire city with the exception of the central business district. To be eligible to receive funds, residents must organize a Neighborhood Priority Board (NPB) whose function is the determination of the priorities for the funding of all grant requests. Residents are free to determine the size and other characteristics of the board. Boards were organized in five areas, and in the sixth area the Model Cities planning council was designated the Neighborhood

Priority Board. The program guidelines require a general consensus for each proposed project or activity, and petitions, public meetings, and field surveys were used to achieve consensus. Limited experience indicates that attendance at an open meeting is the best method for demonstrating consensus.

Several cities are considering various kinds of community councils. The Los Angeles City Charter Commission in July 1969 unveiled a draft charter authorizing the creation, by local initiative, of a neighborhood organization "with an elected board and an appointed neighborman, as a new institutional mechanism for communicating neighborhood needs and goals, involving citizens in city affairs, and reducing feelings of alienation."[14] Neighborhoods would have a population of 5,000 to 30,000. The neighborman would be appointed for an indefinite term by the popularly elected neighborhood board and would be directed to "consider citizens' complaints and seek their resolution with the appropriate public officials and agencies"[15] and assist in the development of neighborhood goals. The city council refused to approve the proposal, and it was not included in the charter submitted to the voters in November 1970. Opponents of the proposal contended that neighborhood organizations would be expensive, might be converted into ward-heeler political systems, and would perform no functions other than those already being performed by the fifteen district councilmen. Minority groups expressed little interest in the proposal.

A somewhat different approach was taken in a Public Administration Service study of city-county consolidation in the Sacramento area in 1957.[16] The study recommended the creation of five borough councils under a consolidated city-county government. A recommendation or request by a borough council would automatically be placed on the agenda of the next metropoiltan council meeting, and each of the five borough councilmen in each borough would serve on one of the key metropolitan commissions—health and welfare, parks and recreation, planning, public safety, and public works. The report also suggested that each borough could have a "sub-city hall" for the provision of services.

In 1970, the Citizens League of Minneapolis proposed the creation of popularly elected community councils within the city.[17] Each council would serve 25,000 to 65,000 residents, and would be formed upon the initiative of neighborhood residents by filing a petition containing five hundred signatures. The league's report pointed out that "the present membership of official elected and appointed boards in many cases does not include representatives of all interests, geographic areas or racial minorities and low-income people in the city." The community councils would have the following powers: appointment of persons to serve on city-wide agencies, review of all proposed city actions affecting their areas, and preparation of plans for the development of their areas.

One of the problems in creating neighborhood councils is the selection of members. No council can reflect all shades of opinion; yet it should be representative of the diverse viewpoints within its neighborhood. When council members are chosen by appointment, the appointing officials experience difficulties in attempting to identify the more alienated citizens who could make a major contribution to the council. A popular election, in some instances, may be a more effective method of selecting members, even though experience in poverty elections revealed little interest in the elections by low-income citizens— as little as 3 to 4 percent of the eligible residents cast ballots. Another complication is that those selected may not continue to remain in close contact with neighborhood views.

In addition to being representative of the neighborhood, a citizen council must be provided with complete information by municipal officials and encouraged to give its frank views with the assurance they will receive full and proper consideration by the city. The National Commission on Urban Problems advised "that the actual policy-making authority needs to be frank in stating the limitations on the authority of the advisory board instead of implying that it has more power than is the case."[18] Citizens will resist the formation of a council whenever they perceive the council to be a cooptative device. And citizens will become disillusioned after electing a council if they discover it does not have all the power they presumed it had. Because a neighborhood council possesses complete freedom to plan and criticize but lacks the power to implement plans, some of the most alienated citizens view a council as tokenism and boycott it.

Although the National Commission on Urban Problems rejected neighborhood government, it did suggest that residents be given "the power to make, or direct, the making of small neighborhood improvements. Examples are addition of more trash receptacles, minor repairs to public property, and tree and flower planting."[19] Little can be said for this recommendation. If residents can be trusted with responsibility for these functions, there is no sound reason why they cannot be entrusted with responsibility for many other functions. Of course, the commission may have selected these minor functions because the cost would be small, economies of scale would not be sacrificed, and municipal unions would not feel threatened.

Ideally, a council should be organized by neighborhood initiative resulting from general and deep-felt citizen concern. Experience indicates, however, that such initiative is rare in disadvantaged neighborhoods except in case of a crisis, such as a proposed project threatening a major demolition and attendant relocation.

Although neighborhood councils have some potential as agents of change, it is questionable whether the councils will play a major role in governing the city in view of the fact they lack staff and are composed of nonexperts. In low-income neighborhoods, it is unrealistic to expect inarticulate citizens to draft plans to solve complex social and economic problems. Unless the councils are provided with advocate planners, their potential lies more in acting as sounding boards for proposals developed by the city's professional staff. It is probably also true that mayors will be more likely to support administrative decentralization rather than neighborhood councils.

Administrative Decentralization

The second major approach adopted by a growing number of large cities to improve the delivery of services on the neighborhood level is administrative decentralization—the dividing of the city into unifunctional or multifunctional administrative districts.

Centralization of power in city hall during the first half of the twentieth century led to congestion in administrative decision making at the top level and the growth of a ponderous bureaucracy. Mayors of large cities increasingly are recognizing that tight centralization of power means they must deal with administrative trivia and cannot respond quickly to rapidly changing conditions in many neighborhoods of the city. Not only do multiple levels of approval slow down the process of administrative decision-making, but the decisions ultimately made tend to be conservative. Thus many mayors have been decentralizing their administrations in order to cut through the bureaucracy and speed up the decision-making process.

The concept of administrative decentralization is a familiar one, for fire stations, police precincts, schools, and many parks have been located on the neighborhood level for many decades. In contrast to a neighborhood government, in which the chief administrative official is responsible to a locally elected council, the director of each administrative district reports to a superior in city hall. Administrative decentralization, however, often provides for the creation of citizen committees to advise the director of each district relative to neighborhood views and wishes.

Administrative decentralization allows many decisions to be made on less than a city-wide basis. Consequently, the scale of government in the eyes of the citizen is reduced, and the coordination of services on the neighborhood level is promoted. Not all functions and services, however, can be decentralized.

The National Commission on Urban Problems in 1968 suggested that the following services could be rendered on the neighborhood level: certain recreation activities, building and housing code inspection, job recruitment, certain job training programs, police-community relations programs, collection of certain fees, complaint bureaus, distribution of food stamps, Head Start program, and public health clinics.[20] The commission also suggested that local residents be hired, where possible, to work in the neighborhood office. This, of course, would necessitate that these positions be exempt from civil service requirements which neighborhood residents could not meet and would undoubtedly generate strong opposition from public employee unions. The commission voted down neighborhood government since this would further fragment decision making and conflict with the commission's recommendation that small units of government be consolidated. Nevertheless, five commission members suggested that neighborhood boards be allowed to perform certain administrative, advisory, and regulatory functions.[21]

Administrative districts, in theory, would help familiarize municipal personnel with conditions in their neighborhoods, promote greater departmental coordination on the district level, provide another access point to government for citizens, and make agencies more responsive to the wishes of their clientele. To maximize interdepartmental coordination, the districts established by each major department should have coterminous boundaries, and district offices of the various departments should be within close proximity of each other.

The amount of discretionary authority possessed by a district office would vary from agency to agency. The building inspection district office, for example, would possess little discretionary authority in contrast to the parks and recreation department's district office, since building safety standards must be uniformly enforced throughout the city while recreation programs can be tailored in large measure to the needs of a district. To ensure that the district administrator has top-level support, he should report directly to the department head. Unless the mayor and department head back the district administrator, decentralization will not accomplish its objectives. The delegation of authority to a district should not be reversed except in extraordinary situations. Should the mayor reverse the decision of the district administrator, it will be apparent that decentralization is an empty shell and that the system remains centralized.

Citizen interest in the district's activities will be greatly influenced by the amount of discretionary authority possessed by a district administrator. Little will be accomplished if community residents agree upon the need for a program and then discover that the local administrator lacks the authority to initiate the desired program. To increase citizen involvement, each district administrator could be authorized to appoint a citizens advisory board. Decentralization will achieve its greatest success in the functions and services heavily dependent upon citizen cooperation, such as parking and traffic regulations, and refuse collection. The city must establish minimum performance standards that all districts must meet and also an appeals mechanism for citizens who believe that the district administrator has acted arbitrarily and capriciously.

The potential for success for a system of administrative decentralization within a large city is dependent upon careful top-level selection of district administrators and continuous evaluation of their performance. Data also must be systematically collected and evaluated in order to provide district administrators with the guidance and information they need to function successfully.

Decentralization of the Police Department. A decentralized approach to improved crime control and police-community relations was inaugurated in Detroit's Tenth Police Precinct with the introduction in 1970 of a Ford Foundation funded Beat Commander System. A beat has a population of approximately 15,000 compared to a precinct population of 130,000. Each Beat Commander Team, composed of twenty-three patrolmen and a sergeant, is assigned permanently to the beat on the assumption that community support for the police would increase and crime prevention would be more effective if the patrolmen came to know the people through attendance at community meetings and personal contact. A preliminary assessment by the Urban Institute—a federally sponsored urban "think tank"—indicates that the new system is achieving the goals of its sponsors.

A similar system was adopted in New York City in 1971 when the police department organized experimental sixteen-member neighborhood teams, equipped with walkie-talkie radios, to patrol twelve square-block areas in Harlem, Brooklyn, Bronx, and Queens. By the following year the number of teams was increased to thirty-eight. Under the neighborhood team concept, the commanding sergeant functions as a neighborhood police chief with authority to modify basic patrol patterns to meet specific problems and situations—a radical change from the old system. The sergeant is responsible for only one sector, but his responsibility is a twenty-four-hour-a-day one. Under the old system, the sergeant in charge of a precinct covering five or six sectors possessed little authority during his eight-hour tour.

On January 19, 1972, Police Commissioner Patrick V. Murphy

extended the neighborhood police team concept by assigning a patrolman who lives in the area to the neighborhood police team. (By tradition, policemen have not been assigned to their own neighborhoods.) The patrolman identifies himself as a "resident patrolman," and he wears gray slacks and a dark blazer with a police patch rather than a uniform. In addition to his routine patrol duties, he solicits the cooperation of his neighbors with the police, advises his team commander relative to neighborhood complaints, and interprets police policy to the neighborhood.

Decentralization in New York City. New York City has a plethora of districts—seventy-five police precincts, fifty-eight sanitation districts, thirty-one school districts, twenty-three health districts, forty-four social service centers, and numerous recreation areas. The overlapping of district boundaries in a crazy-quilt pattern confuses citizens seeking to obtain information or register complaints and frustrates interagency coordination. In most instances, realignment of district boundaries can be accomplished without engendering significant political opposition except that of the bureaucracy.

The organizational problem in New York City is further complicated by a bewildering array of new organizations and programs launched in the 1960's in an attempt to improve communications and the delivery of services—little city halls, neighborhood conservation bureaus, urban action task forces, antipoverty boards, community corporations, community health centers, multiservice centers, and Model Cities advisory boards. In addition, certain areas of the city have well-established, active block associations and political clubs serving local needs and representing the area's views at city hall.

Citizens Union in 1947 recommended that New York City be divided into "nuclear" districts for purposes of planning and decentralizing municipal services; all such services in each district would be grouped in one location. Each district would cover several neighborhoods and, in cooperation with the City Planning Commission, would develop a district plan, modifying it as needed with the passage of time. Implementation of this plan, according to Citizens Union, would improve sensitivity to neighborhood needs and enable the city to "become a great cluster of home towns and still retain the best aspects of its character as the metropolis of the Western World." Acting upon the Citizens Union's recommendations, the City Planning Commission three years later proposed the creation of sixty-six districts responsible for planning for hospitals, housing, libraries, local street systems, playgrounds, schools, and other public facilities and making recommendations relative to land use.

In a joint 1964 report with the Citizens' Housing and Planning

Council, Citizens Union recommended that each city agency with decentralized operations use community districts and work for the development of a community civic center which would promote interagency coordination as well as citizen cooperation and identification with the community. The district administrators might well function as a neighborhood cabinet. The report suggested that the centers could furnish information and handle complaints as well as issue licenses and permits.

On June 4, 1970, Mayor John V. Lindsay recommended that the community boards, discussed earlier in this chapter, be integrated with an expanded number of new "community boards." His proposal for neighborhood government is a form of administrative decentralization and should not be confused with neighborhood government controlled by residents. Under the mayor's plan, each new community board would have a minimum of twenty-four members and a maximum of thirty. The mayor, borough president, and the area councilman each would appoint seven members, and the community school board would appoint three. In addition, a Model Cities advisory committee and a community corporation board operating in the district each could appoint three members. The plan has the obvious advantage of replacing the several existing citizen advisory groups operating in a typical neighborhood with one citizen board.

Each community board would evaluate municipal services, conduct public hearings, make recommendations, work with city officials, and have access to the Office of Neighborhood Government to be established in the mayor's office. A full-time neighborhood director, selected by the mayor from a list submitted by the "community board," would chair meetings attended by officials of city agencies providing services within the district in order to improve administrative coordination and hear citizen complaints. As the mayor's man in the neighborhood and chairman of the community cabinet, the neighborhood director would be in a position to utilize the prestige of the mayor's office in securing the cooperation of city agencies.

An executive assistant of the ·mayor conferred with neighborhood organizations and residents throughout the city in order to obtain their reactions to the plans. He found citizens divided on the method of selecting members of the proposed community boards and recommended that consideration be given to "community boards chosen differently in each community, according to local options." In view of the diversity of the socioeconomic composition of neighborhoods, mixed views on the method of selecting board members, and the desirability of maximizing home rule for neighborhoods, it seemed preferable to allow each neighborhood to devise its own system.

Citizens felt that the mayor's proposed method for selecting the community director deprived them of a major role and that the mayor should automatically appoint the person selected by the community board. The mayor, of course, would not have to accept the recommendations of the community director. The opinion was expressed that the director should "be the community's man to deal with city hall, and not city hall's man to deal with the community." An alternative proposed by many groups was the selection of the director by the community board and the appointment of a second individual by the mayor to function as an *ex officio* member of the board or possibly as chairman of the district's cabinet of agency officials.

On December 22, 1971, Mayor Lindsay announced that five neighborhoods, each corresponding roughly to the boundaries of a community board district, had been selected to test his plan of administrative decentralization. The district directors of eight city agencies—environmental protection, health services, human resources, housing, addiction services, police, parks, and transportation—serve on a neighborhood cabinet chaired by a director selected by the mayor. The district director of each agency has been granted discretionary authority to utilize equipment, personnel, and other resources as he sees fit in order to adapt the services of his agency to the special needs of the district.

Summary

The last half of the 1960's witnessed a period of innovation in big-city administration as mayors sought new ways of maximizing communications with citizens and improving delivery of services on the neighborhood level. Most of the innovations—complaint bureaus, police-community relations programs, little city halls, task forces, neighborhood meetings, neighborhood councils, administrative decentralization—are too recent in origin to permit a final and conclusive judgment as to their effectiveness in achieving their stated objectives. In a number of cities, administrative innovations appear to be functioning reasonably well; in other cities, they have been abandoned or restructured.

Representatives of the disadvantaged and ghetto areas have expressed relatively little opposition to administrative innovations designed to improve neighborhood-city hall communications and the delivery of services on the neighborhood level. They maintain, however, that these innovations are not a substitute for what is really needed —neighborhood control.

Chapter IV

THE ELECTORAL SYSTEM

Most American cities entered the decade of the seventies with institutions fashioned in accordance with the precepts developed in the early decades of the century by the municipal reform movement, which had its base in a growing white middle class. The early reformers wished to clean up corruption, increase the efficiency of municipal government, reduce the influence of political parties, and insulate local issues from state and national ones. They not only promoted strong mayor and council-manager plans but also sought to achieve their objectives by the adoption of at-large voting, nonpartisan elections to insulate local issues, and a small unicameral council. These latter changes, it was assumed, would enable the reformers to recruit and elect a "higher" type candidate to municipal office.

It has become somewhat fashionable to attack the precepts of the municipal reform movement as elitist and designed to politically impoverish the poor; but we should not judge the motives of the early reformers by today's conditions. Intolerable political conditions existed in major cities at the turn of the century, and the reformers did much to improve the caliber of municipal government. Nevertheless, the reform movement has set the stage for a new era of reform, because some of the institutions it shaped have not been sufficiently responsive to the special needs of a sizable segment of a city's population.

The agitation for neighborhood government, as we have seen in Chapter 1, emanates primarily from minority groups convinced that the existing political system neglects their special needs and renders them politically powerless. The at-large electoral system—a product of the municipal reform movement—often produces no direct representation for minority groups; although allowed to vote, they feel that they are effectively disenfranchised by an electoral system that dilutes their voting strength to the point where they are unable to elect a member of the city council or school board. Minority groups can logically ask why should they bother to register and vote when the system apparently is designed to cancel out their votes. To the alienated, the ballot box is not a meaningful form of citizen participation and does not give legitimacy to the city government. The only solution, according to proponents of the colonial analogy, is decolonialization by the creation of neighborhood governments which would allow residents of each neighborhood to control the institutions of local government and their own destinies. A strong case can be advanced, however, that the adoption of an electoral system designed to provide direct representation of disadvantaged minority groups would result in a substantial lessening of the demand for a system of neighborhood government.

The At-Large Electoral System

The various objectives of democratic voting can necessitate different electoral systems. In a referendum, a simple "yes" or "no" vote is sufficient. If only two candidates seek election to an office, allowing voters to cast a vote for one candidate is obviously an adequate system. The situation differs considerably, however, when three or more candidates seek election to an office. Since plurality voting can allow a minority candidate to be elected, some cities hold a run-off election between the two candidates with the largest number of votes in order to guarantee that the candidate elected is the choice of a majority of the voters. A run-off election, unfortunately, has disadvantages of increased cost, probable reduction of voter turnout, and delay. Preferential voting, on the other hand, guarantees the election of a candidate with majority support without the need for a run-off election.

Since democracy means "the rule of the people," few will quarrel with the statement that a democratic government must rest upon the consent of the governed. A problem exists, however, when this concept is applied to a large city. Does the concept mean that a simple majority of all citizens must give their consent, or does it mean a majority in each major neighborhood must give their consent?

Although it must be conceded that at-large elections do not always result in gross underrepresentation of minority groups, a strong case can be made that they usually do not adequately and accurately represent all citizens in cities with a large disadvantaged population. Because generally only candidates who command wide support throughout the city will be elected, at-large elections frequently overrepresent the middle-class majority—in some instances, only a plurality—and often result in no direct representation for minorities who are thus isolated from the center of decision making. George E. Berkley, writing in the *National Civic Review* in 1966, pointed out that the at-large electoral system in Boston produced a council whose members lived in only half of the city's wards. "The rest of the city is effectively shut out from direct representation in the legislative process."[1]

The early municipal reformers, of course, would point out that members of an at-large city council represent voters of the entire city and solicit the votes of citizens regardless of where they live. Nevertheless, members of a minority group often feel they are not properly represented if a member of their group does not serve on the city council or school board. Furthermore, basic policy decisions may be made by a city council unaware of and insensitive to the problems of poor neighborhoods and minority groups. Blacks, for example, frequently state that no white person can adequately represent blacks, because you must be black to understand how blacks feel. Denying the validity of this view does not make it or the alienation associated with it disappear. One would be naive to conclude that blacks will continue to work through an electoral system which provides them with little or no direct representation.

There are hints that at-large elections may be held unconstitutional on the ground that such elections disenfranchise minority groups. In a case involving the Texas legislature, Justice William O. Douglas stated he reserved "decision on one aspect of the problem of multi-member districts. Under the present regime each voter in a district has one vote for each office to be filled. This allows the majority to defeat the minority on all fronts. . . . I am not sure in my own mind how this problem should be resolved."[2]

Blacks recently have filed suits alleging that at-large elections deprive the plaintiffs of their rights under the fourteenth and fifteenth amendments to the United States Constitution. A federal district court in October 1969 ruled that the city of Boston is not under a constitutional compulsion to adopt a ward system as a device to enhance the prospects of a minority group electing its candidates to office, and that "the mere fact that no candidate for whom an elector casts his ballot is successful in the election does not mean that the elector has been unconstitutionally deprived of an effective right to vote."[3] An at-large system, however, might be ruled invalid if it was adopted for the deliberate purpose of reducing the voting influence of a minority group.

Alternative Electoral Systems

The unrepresentativeness of the at-large electoral system has been apparent for many years, but there has been surprisingly little interest in electoral reform. To be properly labeled democratic, a local electoral system must ensure that sizable minorities are able to elect candidates to the city council and school board. Such bodies, representing diverse groups in a heterogeneous city, will be more sensitive to the needs of these groups and better able to engage in the necessary political accommodation. There are several systems, alternative to the at-large electoral system, that will facilitate the election of minority candidates.

Ward Elections—A Form of Limited Voting. Until the early decades of this century, the traditional method used to elect the city council in the United States was ward elections—a system strongly attacked by the municipal reform movement. Richard S. Childs, who worked for the replacement of the system, attributed the demise of ward elections to the following factors:

1. Ward elections confined each voter's influence over the governing body to the single member from his ward. He was denied having anything to say about the majority.
2. Ward elections notoriously produced political small fry who intrigued in the council for petty favors and sought appropriations for their wards in reckless disregard of city-wide interests and the total budget.
3. Ward boundaries got deliberately drawn to favor one faction or party or became obsolete by shifts of population, and redistricting was resisted, sometimes for generations, by the beneficiaries, resulting in gross inequalities of representation and elections of a majority of the council by minorities of the population.
4. The obscurities of ward politics eluded scrutiny by press and public and facilitated development of self-serving political cliques.[4]

Interestingly, ward elections are in accordance with one objective of the municipal reform movement—a short ballot—because each elector has to vote for only one councilman instead of a group of councilmen. Admitting that there is still some validity to Childs' points does not prevent us from re-examining the desirability of utilizing ward elections in place of at-large elections. Today there is growing interest in resurrecting the ward system, especially in large cities, in order to provide representation for all geographical areas of a city.

Coupled with an enlargement of the city council, the restoration of ward elections would provide geographical representation and improve the prospects of minority representation. The enlargement of the council would also reduce the size of councilmanic districts and enable each councilman to keep in closer contact with his constituents, who, in turn, would be better able to judge his performance and to replace him if they are dissatisfied. A related argument in favor of ward elections is that citizens are less hesitant to call upon the councilman for assistance, since they are more likely to know him personally than they would any at-large councilman. This argument is particularly important if the councilman's primary role is viewed as that of an official who performs services for his constituents. On the other hand, this service function can be performed by an information and complaint bureau, as discussed in Chapter 3.

The United States Supreme Court's "one-man, one-vote" ruling should eliminate to a considerable extent the problem of gross inequalities of representation associated in the past with wards of sharply differing populations.[5] However, deliberate gerrymandering is still possible, and silent gerrymandering will occur if ward lines are redrawn only after the decennial federal census. Although substantial enlargement of a city council might facilitate the election of representatives of minority groups, there is the danger that the council may prove to be unwieldy in size, and, hence, result in increased power being exercised by committees considerably less representative of the various elements in the population than the council. Finally, ward elections do not necessarily represent minority groups in proportion to their voting strength, and a geographically dispersed minority may be unable to elect a single candidate to the council or school board. The failure of the ward system to enable large minority groups to elect councilmen is illustrated by the 1969 election in New York City, where no Puerto Rican and only two blacks were elected to the thirty-seven member council in a city where more than 10 percent of the population is Puerto Rican and 17 percent is black.

Combination Ward and At-Large Elections. Recognizing that at-large elections may not provide proper representation for all groups and that ward elections in the past have had undesirable consequences, a number of political observers recommend a combination system which would have the advantages of both at-large and ward elections without their disadvantages. Where this combined system is used, a majority of the councilmen are generally elected at-large to ensure that priority is given to city-wide needs, and a minority is elected on a ward basis to ensure that the special needs of the various neighborhoods are not neglected. A few cities provide for the election of a majority of council members by wards.

At-large elections with district residence requirements have the same objective as combination ward and at-large elections—providing some geographical representation—but the constitutionality of the former has been challenged. In the Virginia Beach consolidation case (the city of Virginia Beach and Princess Anne County had been consolidated) the United States Supreme Court upheld a plan providing for an eleven-member council elected at-large but stipulating that seven members must be residents of specified boroughs.[6.] The boroughs ranged in population from 733 to 29,048. The Court held that the plan made "no distinction on the basis of race, creed, or economic status or location," since all councilmen were elected by all voters of the municipality. The Court also has ruled that it will allow experimentation unless it cancels out "the voting strength of racial or political elements."[7]

At-large elections with residency requirements should help ensure that councilmen have a city-wide constituency and orientation and at the same time a special concern for their individual districts. However, this system will not guarantee that minority groups will be adequately represented.

Limited Nomination and Voting. The failure of the electoral system to provide proper two-party representation in the nineteenth century led to the development and use of limited voting. Under this system, each voter must vote for fewer candidates than there are seats on the city council or school board; the plurality rule determines the winners. As a general rule, limited voting makes it impossible for the largest group or party to win a disproportionate share of the council or board seats and enables the largest minority or party to elect one or more candidates. Voters are not allowed to express preferences, and since each voter gives the same support to the candidate he least favors as to the candidate he most favors, he may contribute to the defeat of his favorite candidate. Consequently, this electoral system encourages bullet voting—voting for only one candidate.

Limited voting may be used in an at-large electoral election or in districts where two or more members are to be elected. New York

City currently uses the system to elect part of its council. No party is allowed to nominate more than one candidate for the two councilman at-large positions in each of the five boroughs, and an elector may not vote for more than one candidate for councilman at-large.[8] Since the adoption of this system in 1963, the Democratic and Republican parties usually have each elected one councilman at-large in each borough. In the 1969 election, three liberals running on the same ticket with Mayor John V. Lindsay were elected councilmen at-large at the expense of the Republican party.

Early court decisions were unfavorable to limited voting. The Rhode Island Supreme Court declared the plan unconstitutional on the ground that the state constitution conferred upon the voters the "right to vote in the election of all civil officers."[9] The New Jersey Court of Errors and Appeal invalidated a law providing for limited nominations,[10] and the New Jersey Supreme Court invalidated a similar law providing for limited voting on the ground that the law violated a provision of the state constitution declaring male citizens over twenty-one eligible "to vote for all elective officers."[11] The Ohio Supreme Court struck down limited voting on the same ground,[12] but in a later case it upheld a form of limited voting, on the ground that a home rule constitutional provision adopted in 1912 gave municipalities all powers of self-government.[13]

The New York State Court of Appeals, the highest court in that state, upheld the constitutionality of limited voting by ruling that the system does not violate the state constitution's provision relative to the qualifications of citizens to vote nor does it violate the fourteenth amendment to the United States Constitution.[14] The United States Supreme Court dismissed an appeal of the New York State decision "for want of a substantial federal question."[15]

The constitutionality of the plan in New York City is still open to question, however, because the United States Supreme Court subsequently ruled that each voter is to be guaranteed a vote of "substantially equal weight to the vote of every other resident."[16] Limited voting meets this criterion for determining constitutionality, provided elections are at-large or districts are of equal population size. The extension of the "one-man, one-vote" concept to local governments raises a question as to the constitutionality of limiting voting in New York City, since the five boroughs vary considerably in population.[17]

Limited voting is a crude method for securing minority representation. It neither guarantees that each group or party will be fully represented in proportion to its voting strength nor prevents a minority from electing a majority of the council members when several strong slates of candidates divide the votes cast. In addition, the system normally provides no representation for independent associations or minority parties other than the largest one. Two hypothetical examples will help illustrate the representativeness of a nine-member council elected by a system restricting each elector to six votes. If the electorate cast 80,000 votes for slate A, 65,000 for slate B, and 55,000 for slate C, slates A and B will win six and three seats respectively. Slate C will not elect a candidate. In other words, a 40 percent minority elects two thirds of the council members. Assuming that a Democratic slate receives 105,000 votes and a Republican slate 95,000, the Democrats with 52.5 percent of the votes will elect six candidates while the Republicans will elect only three candidates.

In a partisan election under limited voting, the majority party may influence the election of a minority councilman by throwing some votes to a favored minority party candidate, thereby encouraging all minority party candidates to curry the favor of the majority party. In a limited-vote election of magistrates in Philadelphia a number of years ago, the majority party divided its supporters into two groups and won both the majority and minority places. Furthermore, there is nothing to prevent the majority party from promoting the formation of slates to divide the opposition vote.

Cumulative Voting. The purpose of cumulative voting—multiple voting for one candidate—is identical to that of limiting voting. Each enables the largest minority group or party to elect one or more members to a city council or school board composed of three or more members. Cumulative voting awards each elector the same number of votes as there are seats on the city council and allows him to give all the votes to one candidate or apportion them among several candidates in accordance with the intensity of his preferences. If a city council has fifteen members, each elector could cast fifteen votes for one candidate, or cast one vote for each of fifteen candidates, or apportion his votes among two or more candidates in any manner that he desires. Provided it is politically cohesive, the minority party can concentrate its votes on one candidate with the expectation that he will be elected.

Cumulative voting attracted considerable attention in the 1870's, and Illinois has used the system since 1870 when the voters approved a constitutional amendment prescribing limited voting for the election of members of the State House of Representatives by three member districts.[18] Cumulative voting was originally adopted to ensure that there would be a strong two-party system by overcoming the sectionalism under which the Democrats won most of the seats in the southern half of the state and the Republicans won most of the seats in the northern half of the state. In the first cumulative voting election, the minority party won a seat in fifty of the fifty-one districts. In 1909, the Illinois Supreme Court ruled that cumulative voting was applicable to primary as well as general elections,[19] and the following year the system was extended to the nomination of representatives.[20]

Although the 1920 and 1970 constitutional conventions voted to abolish cumulative voting, the Illinois electorate decided to continue using the system. Each elector is authorized to cast one vote for each of three candidates, or three votes for one candidate, or one and one half votes for each of two candidates, or two votes for one candidate and one vote for a third candidate. Mathematically, the majority party will be unable to elect three candidates unless it receives over 75 percent of the total votes cast.

Cumulative voting does not guarantee proportional representation, because parties are unable to make their members follow instructions and also miscalculate their strength on occasion. Split-ticket voting alone, if of significant magnitude, will make proportionate representation impossible. Experience in Illinois reveals that the minority party can elect a majority of the members within a district if the majority party miscalculates its strength and nominates three candidates instead of two, thereby splitting its vote and allowing the minority party to elect its two nominees.[21] Since there is an unwritten rule that neither party will nominate more than two candidates, it is the exception when the majority party runs three candidates. Between 1902 and 1970, no district in Illinois had a full slate of six candidates, three nominated by each party; five candidates competed for the three seats in only seventeen elections; and in 99 percent of the elections, either three or four candidates have competed for the three seats. In the 1970 election, only one Senate candidate had no opposition compared to ninety-three House candidates with no opposition. Consequently, there was no pressure to debate the issues in thirty-one districts. It is also possible for a candidate receiving only a small fraction of the total votes cast to be elected. In one district in 1968, a minority party candidate with only 6.4 percent of the votes was elected; the two majority party candidates received 47.6 percent and 45.8 percent respectively of the total votes cast.

The system of cumulative voting has been controversial in Illinois. Many citizens consider it technically complicated and confusing because the ballot can be marked in five different ways and the voter, to be informed, has to follow the activities of three legislators instead of one. Critics also maintain that interparty competition has been eliminated in some districts by so-called "sweetheart deals" and "horse trading" between the two major parties, whereby they agree to nominate a total of three candidates, thus depriving voters of any choice.

In other districts, the two majority party incumbents and the minority incumbent discourage potential challengers by playing down differences and often speaking on each other's behalf.

The lack of party competition could be remedied by requiring each party to nominate at least two candidates, but other problems might be created. If one party has a large majority, it could have some of its members cast votes for the weaker of the minority party's candidates in order to increase the prospects of the majority party winning three seats. The minority party can elect a candidate in such districts only if its members each cast three votes for the same candidate.

Proportional Representation. Concerned about the quality of representation produced by plurality voting in at-large elections, a number of early municipal reformers recommended that the at-large city council and school board be elected by proportional representation. This system of preferential voting is designed to alter the basis of representation by ensuring that various parties and groups are represented, with mathematical exactness, in proportion to their voting strength. In other words, proportional representation attempts to make representative government a reality and allows the voter to express more completely his judgment of the relative qualifications of candidates. Our discussion of proportional representation will be limited to the single transferable vote system developed by Thomas Hare of London in 1857.

In a proportional representation election, voters indicate a graduation of preferences for candidates by placing a number next to each candidate's name. A "1" is placed opposite the candidate of the first choice, a "2" opposite the second-choice candidate, and so on; the voter may indicate as many choices as he desires. To be elected, a candidate must receive a number of votes equal to the quota, which is determined by dividing the total number of valid ballots by the number of councilmen to be elected plus one, plus one ballot. If 100,000 valid ballots are cast to elect a nine-member city council, the quota would be equal to

$$\frac{100,000}{\text{No. of councilmen} + 1} + 1 = 10,001.$$ This formula always produces the

smallest number of votes that will absolutely assure a candidate's election no matter how the votes may be distributed among the candidates.

Following the determination of the quota, the ballots are sorted by first choices. If any candidate receives a total of number "1" ballots equal to or exceeding the quota, he is declared elected. Should a candidate receive more than the quota, his surplus ballots are divided among the other candidates according to the second choices indicated. The next step in the count of the ballots is to declare defeated the candidate with the fewest number "1" votes and any surplus votes transferred from candidates already elected and to distribute his ballots to the other candidates according to the next choices marked on them. If the second choice already has been elected or defeated, the ballots are distributed according to the third choice. A new count is conducted, and any candidate who has a total of number "1" and transferred ballots equal to or exceeding the quota is declared elected. His surplus, if any, is distributed to the remaining candidates. The process of declaring defeated the lowest candidate and transferring his ballots to the remaining candidates as indicated by the next choice on the ballots is continued until the full council or school board is elected. Candidates usually are not allowed to exceed the quota during a transfer; upon reaching the quota, any surplus ballots are immediately given to the next choice before the tabulation of new totals. Most ballots, either on the first choice or by transfer, help elect a candidate.

Either the Toledo or the Boulder system is used to govern the transfer of surplus ballots. Under the Toledo system, the quota is determined before the ballots are distributed to their first choices. As soon as a candidate receives enough number "1" ballots to reach the quota, these ballots are locked up, and any subsequent number "1" ballots for this candidate are automatically transferred to the number "2" choice. Under the Boulder system, surplus number "1" votes are distributed according to a formula. The ballots of a candidate receiving a surplus of number "1" votes are re-examined to determine the distribution of number "2" votes. The surplus ballots are then distributed proportionally according to second choices. If candidate X received 12,000 number "1" ballots and the quota is 10,000, he has a surplus of 2,000. Assuming that candidate Y was the number "2" choice on 6,000 of candidate X's number "1" ballots, candidate Y would be given one half of the surplus or 1,000 ballots.

The principal advantage of proportional representation is that it assures majority rule while guaranteeing minority representation. Proportional representation recognizes that in a modern city there are numerous factional divisions, and the system makes it impossible for any political party or faction with a slight electoral majority to elect all members of a city council or school board. For example, in the 1949 New York election on a district basis under plurality voting, the Democrats captured twenty-four of the twenty-five city council seats while polling only 52.6 percent of the votes cast. Had proportional representation been in effect, the party division would have been quite different: thirteen Democrats, six Republicans, three Liberals, and three American Labor Party members. In contrast to ward elections, a geographically dispersed minority will be able to elect a candidate under proportional representation, since the constituency is based on interest rather than residence. The strength of a minority group is not dissipated if it gives most of its number "1" votes to one of its candidates or scatters its votes among several of its candidates. While a minority group will be fully represented under proportional representation, it cannot benefit from a split among opposition groups, as under limited voting and cumulative voting, and elect a majority of the members of a council or school board. Although proportional representation is often advocated because it provides representation for minority parties, it also enables the majority party to gain seats—in contrast with ward elections—if the majority party members are concentrated in a few wards.

In addition to providing minorities with representation, the at-large use of proportional representation has several other advantages. Under a plurality system, a popular name at the head of a party column can carry weak or unqualified candidates into office; this cannot happen under proportional representation. Consequently, the services of an able councilman will not necessarily be lost if his party fails to win a plurality or a majority, for proportional representation will enable him to win re-election. If the election is nonpartisan, proportional representation will facilitate the election of independent candidates who otherwise might not seek election.

Proportional representation at-large makes gerrymandering impossible, since there are no district lines to be gerrymandered. It also guarantees a relatively large turnout of the eligible voters compared to the turnout in a primary election. A small voter turnout facilitates control of candidate nomination by a machine or small clique, particularly if the opposition is divided. Regardless of the size of the voter turnout, the effect of division is less under proportional representation because of the transferable vote. In their analysis of the use of proportional representation in New York City elections, Belle Zeller and Hugh A. Bone concluded that it "forced higher caliber candidates on both the majority and minority political organizations."[22]

The possibility of election frauds is reduced by proportional representation. The selection of councilmen by districts and plurality voting tempts unscrupulous individuals to purchase votes or influence the counting of ballots in districts where the election is close. Since proportional representation is based on at-large voting and ballots are centrally counted by expert tellers under close supervision, the influence of any purchased votes is reduced and the possibility of tampering with the counting of ballots is minimized. Startling irregularities in the count of proportional representation ballots are unknown.

Bullet voting is common in at-large voting, as we have seen, because additional choices might help defeat a group's candidate. In a proportional representation election, second and subsequent choices are looked at only if the first choice has been elected or defeated. Consequently, the presence of many preferences on the ballot has no effect on the prospect of the first choice being elected.

Proportional representation can promote cooperation among members of local governing bodies. George H. Hallett, Jr., has pointed out that "instead of trying to beat a particular person, with the temptation to belittle his ability and blacken his character, each candidate is trying to win a group of supporters for himself out of the whole field. He knows that he cannot defeat the leaders of the opposition. . . . His best course is to make a vigorous statement of what he himself stands for, without gratuitous attack on anyone else."[23]

In spite of the advantages proportional representation offers, campaigns to secure its adoption have been marked by strong emotional opposition. Among other things, proportional representation is indicted as un-American because it is of foreign origin. This charge can be readily dismissed as spurious. Another emotional charge against proportional representation is that it permitted the election of two Communists and two American Labor Party candidates to the New York City council in 1945. These two parties accounted for 18 percent of the first choice votes and received 17.5 percent of the council seats. One must remember that this election occurred at a time when the Soviet Union was a friendly ally that recently had helped the United States to defeat Nazi Germany. A Communist could not be elected to a city council in the United States today under proportional representation or any other democratic electoral system.

Proportional representation, according to its opponents, promotes civic disunity and strife by fostering splinter groups and emphasizing ethnic, racial, and religious politics in contrast with a "good" electoral system which plays down divisive prejudices. A system that shuts out minority groups, however, does not play down divisive prejudices but does aggravate alienation. Furthermore, there is no evidence that voting along ethnic, racial, and religious lines is any more common under proportional representation than under other electoral systems.

Although one may concede that proportional representation facilitates the election of minority candidates, the objection is raised that it does not guarantee that each neighborhood will be represented on the city council and school board. As under regular at-large elections, all councilmen and school board members elected by proportional representation theoretically might live in the same section of the city. This has never occurred.

The counting of paper ballots cast in a proportional representation election in a large city requires several days—nine days, for example, in the 1939 New York City election. One should not lose sight of the fact that proper representation is more important than the speedy count of ballots. Since most councils and school boards are elected in November and do not take office until January, there is no valid reason why the results of the election must be known immediately. The use of voting machines or computer cards, on which work is now progressing, can completely overcome this objection to proportional representation.

The cost of counting paper ballots used in a proportional representation election is greater than the cost of counting ballots in a regular municipal election. However, proportional representation saves the cost of a primary election, and the use of voting machines or computer cards will probably reduce the cost of counting ballots in a proportional representation election.

Experience indicates that the ballot tends to be long in the first proportional representation election—152 candidates for 9 city council seats in the first proportional representation election in Worcester, Massachusetts, in 1949—but in subsequent elections it soon becomes relatively short as potential candidates recognize they need substantial voter support to be elected. In any event, voters under proportional representation do not have to know or vote for all candidates. A voter who marks his first seven to ten preferences will in most cases help elect one of these candidates because of the transferable ballot.

The major argument advanced in opposition to proportional representation is that it is a fantastically complicated system understood by relatively few citizens. Proponents of proportional representation point out that the mechanics of voting are simple. In the 1970 community school board elections in New York City, for example, the percentage of invalid ballots was only 2.5 percent, and in most districts the blank ballots were less than one fifth of 1 percent of the total ballots cast. Proponents also claim that the system works and that the method of counting the ballots, although complicated, does not have to be completely understood by every citizen. George H. Hallett, Jr., dismisses the charge that proportional representation is a complicated system by use of analogies.

> The comparative complexity of the Hare system count is a matter of trifling concern to the intelligent voter. He does not have to count the ballots any more than he has to make his own watch or repair his own car. The watch is more complicated than the sun dial and the car than the stage coach, but they give better results.[24]

Proportional representation has apparently been given a new lease on life recently because of the demands that black and Puerto Rican minorities be given direct representation on city councils and school boards. Of the 279 school board members elected under proportional representation in New York City in 1970, seventy-seven were black or Puerto Rican. Forty-four of the seventy-seven were elected in six of the thirty-one districts, and the remainder in fifteen of the other twenty-five districts. While this was not in full proportion to the black and Puerto Rican population, it was strikingly better than the results in New York City elections under other electoral systems. The voter turnout—14 percent of the eligible voters—was about average for school board elections not held in conjunction with general municipal elections. However, the boycott of the elections by some militant blacks and Puerto Ricans who favor complete community control of the schools resulted in the elections of boards not fully representative of these groups.

Summary

The at-large electoral system employed in a majority of American cities fails to provide sizable minority groups with direct representation on the city council and school board. Some members of these groups, therefore, have concluded that the act of voting is a pointless exercise, since the electoral system effectively cancels their votes. A system of neighborhood government, on the other hand, would enable geographically concentrated minorities to elect their candidates and control the instruments of power in their neighborhoods.

Our survey of alternative electoral systems—ward elections, combination ward and at-large elections, limited voting, cumulative voting, and proportional representation—reveals that each system has the potential for facilitating the election of minority candidates but that only proportional representation will represent minority groups in direct proportion to their voting strength. Adoption of this electoral system would revitalize city government and reduce the demand for a system of neighborhood government.

Chapter V

THE FEDERATED CITY

The failure of large cities to deliver quality services to neighborhoods and the inability of citizens to effectively influence municipal policy through administrative and electoral channels are the root causes of the movement for the establishment of a federated city by the creation of neighborhood governments. In a federated system—also characterized as a two-tier system—the city government or upper-tier would retain complete control over services that need to be provided on a large territorial basis, and neighborhood or lower-tier governments would be responsible for functions that are closest to the people. In other words, the city government would control a number of delivery systems and neighborhood governments would control other delivery systems. Responsibility for certain functions would be shared by the two levels of government.

The new reformers have examined the reasons for the failure of the municipal government to provide quality services and have concluded that the failure is attributable to an overcentralized bureaucracy which ignores, partially or completely, neighborhood wishes and desires. In their view, the solution must involve an institutional change that will increase public officials' accountability to neighborhood residents by allowing them to control the instruments of government, including the delivery system in their neighborhoods. This control would include, among other things, the power to prepare a neighborhood budget, tax, borrow funds, and hire and fire personnel. Although proponents of neighborhood government have oversimplified the reason why municipal governments have failed to deliver quality services in disadvantaged neighborhoods, one can still give serious consideration to their proposal for a system of neighborhood governments.

Based upon the analysis contained in the preceding chapters, a positive approach to the reform of large city government in the United States would involve the conversion of the existing unitary system into a federation, improvement of city hall-neighborhood communications, decentralized delivery of services by the upper-tier government where possible, and adoption of proportional representation. Political and administrative decentralization should prove beneficial by increasing the number of access points for citizens seeking to influence policy making in a large city. To avoid fragmentation on the neighborhood level, single-purpose governmental entities should be avoided. Each neighborhood government should have a population in the range of 25,000 to 250,000 and initially should be assigned responsibility for schools, libraries, health services, social services including day-care programs, and neighborhood parks and recreational programs.

Neighborhood Government

The United States has had a considerable amount of experience with extralegal forms of neighborhood government—settlement houses in low-income areas and neighborhood associations in middle-class areas—but experience with the type of neighborhood government demanded by the new breed of reformers in large cities is limited to community school districts in Detroit and New York City and to neighborhood corporations funded by the Office of Economic Opportunity. Rational analysis of the potential of a system of neighborhood government is, unfortunately, hindered by the very limited amount of experience with it and the emotional rhetoric of the many claims and counterclaims about the system.

The Positive View. Neighborhood government is justified primarily on noneconomic grounds. By facilitating more citizen inputs into the decision-making process in a large city, a system of multifunctional neighborhood governments, it is contended, will make local government more responsive to the special needs of citizens in different neighborhoods and will help legitimatize government in alienated neighborhoods. In particular, popular support for the Marxist colonial analogy should dissipate. This argument appears to be reasonable. Policy outcomes should be different if decisions in certain functional areas are made by elected neighborhood councils rather than by the city council. Uniform city-wide policies would be replaced by policies custom-tailored to the conditions prevailing in each neighborhood, and procedures should be more flexible since the territorial base is smaller. Administrators employed by a neighborhood government should become intimately familiar with community leaders and problems. This familiarity should make each administrator more sympathetic to the special needs and desires of neighborhood residents, resulting in a lowering of tension between citizens and the bureaucracy.

Advocates of community control maintain that a system of neighborhood government will prove beneficial in ghetto neighborhoods by restoring a sense of community. Unfortunately, this contention has little empirical support. The highly mobile population and relatively large size of proposed neighborhood governments—a population as great as 250,000—would make the development of a deep-felt sense of community impossible. The theory of neighborhood government is based upon the assumption that there is a coalescence of common interests within a definable geographical territory. It is apparent, however, that conflict may be more prevalent than a commonality of interests in many neighborhoods. Micropolitan governments, however, may be able to manage urban conflict more successfully than the present city government, thereby promoting political stability.

Proponents suggest that neighborhood governments will revitalize democracy on the local level by restoring consent of the governed and dramatically increasing citizen participation in disadvantaged neighborhoods. This belief, unfortunately, is wishful thinking, for low citizen participation is a fact of political life, particularly among disadvantaged citizens. As the locus of authority in a large city is converted into multiple loci with the devolution of political power, citizens will be able to identify more readily with neighborhood governments because of their smaller scale, and this identification may take the form of greater citizen participation. We would be deceiving ourselves, however, if we concluded that town meeting democracy could be replicated on the neighborhood level in large cities, as suggested by Kotler.[1] Nevertheless, institutional changes that lower barriers to citizen participation by offering citizens new access points to the centers of decision making should be supported.

A system of neighborhood government would in theory relieve the mayor, councilmen, and administrators of minutia and headaches resulting from neighborhood pressure for action to solve particular problems, absolve them of blame for administrative failures in programs turned over to the neighborhood governments, and give them more time to devote to city-wide concerns. The mayor of a large city plays a major role in minimizing political conflict because his tenure in office is dependent upon maintaining a broad coalition of support; this coalition would be ruptured if his administration took action highly advantageous to one group and disadvantageous to another group. Racial polarization in some cities has made conflict resolution by the mayor nearly impossible. Neighborhood government may be a partial way out of the impasse, for the new power relationships inherent in such a system might enable the mayor to avoid certain issues entirely or partially. That this will occur is unlikely. The mayor in council-manager cities, for example, is only the presiding officer of the city council and ceremonial head of the city, yet many citizens view him as the chief executive. Citizens in a federated city will undoubtedly continue to pressure the mayor to marshal the city's resources to solve particular neighborhood problems.

The Negative View. Critics have advanced a series of objections to the creation of a system of neighborhood governments. They suggest that such a system will resurrect parochialism, result in the neglect of city-wide concerns, and lead to the eventual dismemberment of the city. This argument can be safely rejected, provided the city-wide government of a federated city is given adequate authority and finances to perform its assigned functions. The fact that neighborhood governments would encourage residents to concentrate on problems in their respective neighborhoods may be viewed as a type of parochialism; but it should be viewed as a natural and healthy manifestation of citizen concern with public problems. By encouraging citizens to participate in the solution of community problems, a system of neighborhood government may also encourage some citizens to develop interest in city-wide and metropolitan problems.

During the 1960's ethnic and racial differences were sharpened dramatically, causing a social upheaval in many major cities. The situation has grown more explosive as blacks and other minority groups have become more militant, and their demand for community control of hospitals, schools, and other institutions appears as a threat to members of the white middle class. The creation of neighborhood governments as full-fledged municipalities might sharpen ethnic and racial cleavages and intensify segregation. Not only might white neighborhoods exercise governmental power to exclude blacks, but black neighborhoods might use similar powers to exclude whites. As we pointed out in Chapter 1, black separatists maintain that suburban communities are neighborhood governments wielding power to preserve lily-white enclaves and that blacks should be in a position to preserve similar enclaves in the inner city.

Daniel P. Moynihan, an astute urban observer, has written that forcing the mayor "to break up his administration into endless fractionating units will bring on anarchism at best and chaos at worst. Given the heterogeneous political community of most cities, this potential for ethnic and racial chaos . . . is especially great."[2] Struggles between blacks and Spanish-speaking residents for control of multiservice centers, community corporations, and Model Cities programs in Chicago, Los Angeles, New York City, and San Francisco appear to lend support to Moynihan's view. Nevertheless, we believe his view greatly overstates the danger that a system of neighborhood government will produce ethnic and racial chaos. Friction between ethnic and racial groups is nothing new in this country, and aggravation of such friction is not so serious a danger as the potential for conflict inherent in deeply alienated neighborhoods. The civil disorders of the mid-1960's brought into clear perspective the powder kegs produced by political alienation in a period of rising expectations. We agree with Altshuler that community control tends to be conducive to racial peace.[3] A black-controlled neighborhood government, for example, would not be accused by blacks of taking action based upon racial prejudice.

Black control, however, does not necessarily mean that the conflict will be absent in a neighborhood. To cite only one example, Community School District 23 in New York City has been a center of conflict, but the participants in the conflict are not divided along racial lines. The division is between those controlling the community school board and those who formerly controlled the Ocean Hill-Brownsville demonstration school district.

Boundaries for neighborhood governments, moreover, do not have to be drawn on the basis of racial concentration in all instances. Most central cities have a number of racially mixed neighborhoods, and the probability of a neighborhood being all black or all white diminishes as its area and population are increased.

Fear of discrimination and tyranny of the majority may be prevalent among members of a minority ethnic or racial group as a neighborhood government is being formed, and they may conclude that they should flee to a neighborhood where they would be in the majority. This fear, however, is without substantial foundation for four principal reasons. First, there are federal and state statutes outlawing the more flagrant forms of discrimination. Second, the establishment of a federated city would obviate the possibility of neighborhood discrimination against a minority in those functional areas designated as the sole or shared responsibility of the city-wide government. Third, adoption of proportional representation would guarantee a racial or ethnic minority direct representation on the neighborhood council, thereby enabling the minority to protect its interests. Finally, leaders of neighborhood governments generally will be moderates, as the community school board elections in New York City demonstrated. Militants are reluctant to seek elected office and usually are defeated when they so do. If they are elected, the responsibilities of office tend to have a sobering effect. Consequently, it is unreasonable to conclude that a neighborhood government could be truly racist even if the leaders of the majority favored a policy of racism.

There is, of course, the danger that neighborhood governments in ghetto areas will be controlled by minorities should most voters fail to exercise their franchise at the polls. The poverty elections in the mid-1960's and the New York community school board elections in 1970 had low voter participation. Less than 5 percent of the eligible voters typically participated in poverty elections, and approximately 14 percent participated in the community school board elections. The low voter turnout in poverty elections is not surprising since the stakes were not high. The stakes in the community school board elections were higher, and this partially accounts for the larger voter turnout. Stakes would be considerably higher if multifunctional neighborhood governments were created, and voter turnout would probably be correspondingly higher.

Critics maintain that neighborhood governments in disadvantaged areas will be less innovative than the existing municipal government. It is unlikely that ghetto residents will be able, on the basis of their limited education and experience, to develop innovations that will be more beneficial than innovations developed by professionals. Nevertheless, ghetto residents are convinced that the traditional methods of providing services have been a failure and therefore are likely to be willing to try innovations.

Doubts are raised as to whether sufficient leadership exists in ghetto areas to enable micropolitan governments to function successfully and survive. Residents of such areas tend to lack training, and many are burdened with individual and collective problems of great magnitude. Yet leaders can be developed and trained as the antipoverty program demonstrated. The task of developing leadership in ghetto neighborhoods is a huge one, and federal, state, and local governments as well as private organizations would have to provide considerable technical assistance.

Will the creation of neighborhood governments magnify the problem of governmental corruption? This question is especially pertinent since supporters of community control center much of their fire on professionalism, and one may draw the conclusion that traditional professional values—honesty, efficiency, neutral competence—would be played down by neighborhood governments, and responsiveness would be stressed. Experience with certain antipoverty agencies—Harlem Youth Opportunities Unlimited and Associated Community Teams HARYOU-ACT) in New York City and Action for Boston Community Development (ABCD), for example—appears to support an affirmative answer to the question of increased corruption. The corruption associated with the antipoverty program in its early years, however, resulted from haste in launching the program and failure to adopt proper control procedures. Greater care should be exercised if a decision is made to launch a system of neighborhood governments. State governments, which played no role in creating the local antipoverty agencies, would supervise the creation of neighborhood governments as they did when community school districts were created in Detroit and New York City. To date, there has been no corruption associated with either community school system. Furthermore, city governments have not been free of corruption, and evidence is lacking to support the conclusion that corruption is positively correlated with small governmental units.

The charge is also advanced that economies of scale would be lost by the creation of a system of neighborhood government. If a federated city plan is adopted, the functions benefiting the most from economies of scale probably would be assigned to the upper-tier government. Furthermore, neighborhood performance of certain governmental functions does not necessarily mean that economies of scale are being forfeited. The neighborhood governments proposed in cities such as Chicago and New York City would be large ones; each would have a population of approximately 250,000 and be larger than all but fifty-one of our cities. Neighborhood units of this size should be able to benefit from economies of scale in providing most services. As we saw in Chapter 1, an Advisory Commission on Intergovernmental Relations study found the size of a city in the population range of 25,000 to 250,000 has no significant relationship to economies or diseconomies of scale; significant diseconomies of scale are encountered as size exceeds 250,000, however, because of the law of diminishing returns. One should also keep in mind that efficiency may be improved in terms of faster provision of services in response to neighborhood requests and complaints.

Opponents state that micropolitan governments would deprive the mayor of flexibility in responding to emergency situations in a given area since he would no longer be in a position to marshal and direct the total resources of the city. There can be no denying that the mayor would be unable to direct the resources associated with functions that have been assigned to neighborhood governments, but in an emergency situation it is probable that the type of assistance needed in a given area could be provided by agencies under the mayor's control. One should not forget that the state and federal governments also are called upon to render assistance in emergency situations.

Administrative Reform

The second aspect of our model for the revitalization of large city government is administrative reform designed to improve neighborhood-city hall communications and the delivery of services on the neighborhood level. The administrative experiments—little city halls, complaint bureaus, neighborhood meetings, neighborhood councils, and administrative decentralization—were described in Chapter 3. These experiments are premised on the belief that improved communications, coupled with decentralized delivery of services, would help bridge the gap between citizen and government and improve the delivery of services on the neighborhood level, thereby dissipating political alienation.

Most of these innovations are relatively new, and their effectiveness has not been systematically analyzed. A 1971 survey of 470 cities over 25,000 population, conducted by the Advisory Commission on Intergovernmental Relations and the National League of Cities, reveals that 72 percent of the top city officials responding believe that the innovations have been "a difficult but very worthwhile experience resulting in increased trust and understanding between citizens, city hall officials, and public administrators."[4] Unfortunately, no similar survey of citizens has been conducted to determine their assessment of the accomplishments of administrative reforms.

The strongest criticism of little city halls comes from Milton Kotler, the leading publicist for neighborhood government:

There are different intentions in the advocacy of little city halls. At one level, it is supposed that community power can achieve its demands if public administration is decentralized in the neighborhoods. The closer contact between the neighborhood and city administration would ensure a better delivery of services that people need. But this is a superficial view, since no decentralization of an administration which is based on a government that aims to rule the neighborhoods for the interests of downtown will ever have the resources or disposition to deliver public services to any equitable and just degree. Hence, little city halls, under the present oligarchic rule of our cities, will only turn into improved police bastions in the neighborhoods.[5]

Having fully accepted the Marxist colonial analogy, Kotler has no choice but to conclude that any administrative change, such as the introduction of little city halls, is a scheme to increase the control of the "mother country" or central business district over its "colonies"— the ghetto neighborhoods. Little city halls have not been utilized in any city as "police bastions," and no public official has advocated such a use. In Chapter 3, we pointed out that police departments have launched community relations programs in ghetto neighborhoods by opening offices to reduce friction with the community by facilitating communications and promoting public understanding of the role of the police. These offices have not been utilized as "police bastions," nor have they been used as police precinct headquarters, in spite of the fact that many neighborhood residents view the offices as precinct headquarters.

Kotler adds that "there is also a better intention" associated with the advocacy of "little city halls."[6] He stated that "thoughtful liberals" desire to shift political power from the oligarchs to a new class of professional bureaucrats. He continues by stating that the halls will help increase the political power of professional bureaucrats in relation to downtown power and will "also be local terminals of planning and just city service." Kotler rejects this better intention on two grounds:

> First, while it is conceivable that the new class of adminis-
> trators could run a good government were they to triumph over
> the present oligarchic power of downtown, there is no reason for
> the neighborhoods either to assume their triumph or to trust their
> goodness. . . . Secondly, it is a mistake to think that the political
> object of the present movement of neighborhood power is better
> services, for men primarily desire the liberty of local rule and
> democratic decision. On this score, the mere promise of political
> influence to the neighborhoods in the planning process and admin-
> istration is no substitute for empowering them to actually implement
> local decisions.[7]

Kotler, of course, is correct in concluding that public adminis-
trators in charge of neighborhood city halls possess little political power. To date, little real power has been delegated to the halls since they serve primarily as information and complaint centers. The movement

for administrative decentralization, on the other hand, is premised upon the delegation of substantial power to the administrators of muncipal programs in various neighborhoods in order to make the agencies more responsive to the wishes of the community. There is no evidence to support Kotler's conclusion that local rule is desired more strongly by neighborhood residents than better services. Pressures for community control emanate primarily from the failure to deliver adequate munic-ipal services on the neighborhood level.

Administrative decentralization is a proven method for the effi-cient delivery of services on the neighborhood level in large cities. Problems, however, are associated with a decentralized operation, as Howard W. Hallman has pointed out:

> Since it is exceedingly rare for the central unit responsible for budgeting, personnel, or purchasing to completely relinquish con-trol of its function to a field unit, the field personnel involved in these tasks will have divided responsibility. They will be respon-sible to the director of field operations for some matters and to the central specialist in others. This is the traditional "two masters" situation, a classic problem in administration.[8]

A related problem results from neighborhood pressure to persuade field officials to act as advocates on behalf of the local community. In many instances, officials responsible for decentralized services in a neighborhood can act as advocates without entering into a conflict with superiors. In other instances, the field personnel may be out of sym-pathy with central policy but have no alternative but to implement it or resign. These problems may be most serious for field adminis-trators in disadvantaged neighborhoods—particularly if the advisory board is composed of militants—but they need not negate the advan-tages of decentralization.

Perhaps the most serious problem associated with city hall's attempt to improve communications with neighborhoods and the delivery of services in large cities involves the plethora of citizen organizations and delivery structures that have been created—little city halls, multiservice centers, police-community relations units, community planning boards, neighborhood councils, and numerous overlapping administrative districts. Adding to this confusing array of organizations, which divide the energy and talents of citizens, are federally sponsored urban renewal Project Area Committees, antipoverty boards, and Model Cities ad-visory boards. In addition, many neighborhoods have block associations, improvement associations, and political clubs established many years ago. A great need exists for a consolidation of neighborhood citizen organizations in order to make the most effective use of citizen talents and allow residents to have one source of information and one mechanism through which to express their views. A single neighborhood council, by means of committees, could perform many of the functions currently handled by existing citizen organizations.

Proportional Representation

Administrative changes, no matter how desirable, are ameliorative devices and cannot end political alienation that is the product of an unrepresentative electoral system. As we indicated in Chapter 4, there is a palpable need for more representative local governments, and reform of the electoral system must be a key ingredient of any program for revitalizing large city government. Although the introduction of ward elections, combination ward and at-large elections, at-large elections with residency requirements, limited voting, or cumulative voting will improve the prospects for members of minority groups to win elections, only proportional representation will guarantee that the city council and school board will represent all minority groups in the city in direct proportion to their voting strength. Proportional representation, however, cannot guarantee that the representatives of minority groups will be able to influence the decisions of the council and school board, since the majority can always outvote the minority.

Proportional representation will not maximize citizen participation overnight. Voter registration and the number of votes cast will not increase sharply in ghetto areas following the initial use of proportional representation because deep-rooted alienation cannot be quickly and easily eliminated. To many ghetto residents, the substitution of proportional representation for the existing electoral system may appear to be another middle-class scheme to keep them politically suppressed. Only when the ghetto leaders perceive that proportional representation will perform as promised will political participation increase significantly.

Reform of the electoral system as advocated will mean that fewer middle-income persons and more low-income persons will be elected to the city council and school board. The legislative process may become more difficult under proportional representation because more compromises will be necessary in order to reconcile the conflicting interests of the various groups of citizens represented by the councilmen. On the other hand, the quality of local legislation should improve when the needs and views of all citizens are represented on the council. Decisions will be made by a majority of the councilmen as usual, but the composition of the majority will not be identical on as many issues as when members were elected at-large.

Not surprisingly, middle-class members of the city council and school board will discover that it is difficult to win the support of lower-class members for projects that are considered to be of "city-wide" importance. However, if a genuine high priority need exists, these members can be convinced of the importance of a "city-wide" project by frank discussion. They will also see to it that the needs of their constituents and areas are not neglected by an undue emphasis on "city-wide" needs.

The mayor also may experience more difficulty in winning council support for his program and may have to make concessions to groups and areas which he often could ignore in the past. If his policies have broad appeal, he may fare better with a more representative council than with one overrepresentative of the white middle class. Mayor Fiorella H. LaGuardia of New York City wrote that the city council elected by proportional representation has "been annoying and exasperating," but he added: "Is not every executive subjected to criticism, or even, if you please, to be harassed by the legislative body? I am glad that I am living under a system of government that permits an executive to be criticized, even if that criticism extends to the point of unjustifiable abuse."[9] If the mayor is successful in persuading minority group councilmen of the importance of his program, their support will facilitate its implementation in minority group areas by ensuring the cooperation of the residents.

A positive correlation exists between the type of electoral system employed and the responsiveness of a unit of local government to its citizens. The changed socioeconomic composition of the population of central cities makes it imperative to replace a system favoring the middle class with a more representative system that will strengthen participatory democracy by encouraging citizens to play a role in the political life of the city. Although the adoption of proportional representation is not advocated as a substitute for neighborhood government, responsiveness would flow out of representativeness, thereby reducing the pressures for the creation of neighborhood governments.

Political Support for Change

Evidence is lacking that a majority of the residents in any neighborhood favor complete secession from the city. Support for the creation of a federal system, however, is growing. To date, the strongest support for the creation of a system of neighborhood government is found in black ghettos where many residents have abandoned their quest for integration. They now favor structural changes designed to allow them to control certain governmental functions in their neighborhoods and free them from what they consider to be the tyranny of a paternalistic bureaucracy centered in city hall. Will mayors, councilmen, and bureaucrats support or thwart citizen efforts aimed at the establishment of a system of neighborhood government?

Kotler, a leading advocate of neighborhood government, contends that the mayor will favor the devolution of political power to neighborhoods because this will increase his authority.

> The wise mayor, who gives authority for self-rule to the communities, will gain not only the votes of a grateful community, but also their understanding that their local authority depends on his continued strength. Further, the mayor will discover that the neighborhood corporation is an efficient and stable unit with which to negotiate.[10]

The typical mayor probably will be reluctant to strongly support the devolution of authority to neighborhood governments, for he will want to retain his power of review. In Chapter 3, we pointed out that Mayor John V. Lindsay's plan for neighborhood government is actually a plan for administrative decentralization. Not one mayor of a large city has publicly declared himself in favor of community control of the major municipal functions. In other words, mayors favor administrative decentralization and improved communications rather than political decentralization.

To accomplish their objectives, neighborhood governments must be adequately financed. As recommended in Chapter 1, a neighborhood government should be authorized to levy user charges and property, income, and sales taxes. These taxes might be collected by the city, county, or state. Furthermore, a neighborhood government should not be burdened with restrictive tax and debt limits but should be made eligible to receive federal and state grants-in-aid.

Prospects that mayors and city councilmen will provide neighborhood governments with greatly expanded financial resources with no strings attached are nil. Hard-pressed for funds themselves, these officials will be reluctant to allocate scarce fiscal resources to functions not directly under their control. If they decide to fund neighborhood governments, they will want to maintain control over the alloted funds, including the right to terminate funds if they are improperly utilized. Mayors and other municipal officials might be more receptive to funding neighborhood governments if the enabling legislation contained a provision that whenever a neighborhood government fails to meet prescribed performance standards, city officials would operate the neighborhood government on a temporary basis until conditions improved.

An at-large city council may be more sympathetic to the creation of neighborhood governments than one elected on a ward basis, because the new system would enable the council to continue to focus its attention on city-wide issues. A ward councilman probably would oppose an institutional change that might diminish his power and influence in his area of the city. But he might actively support a system of neighborhood government if he was designated the chairman of the neighborhood council or if the governing body of each neighborhood included the ward councilmen elected in the area as *ex officio* members.

With respect to the position of municipal unions toward neighborhood government, Altshuler writes:

> . . . a strong case can be made that community control would strengthen rather than weaken them [unions] as institutions. If one examines the history of labor-management relations, few lessons are so clear as that the potential for union dominance is greatest where one union faces numerous employers. In this situation, it can generally pursue a "whipsaw" strategy, focusing its attack upon a single employer at contract time, assuming that if he gives in the others will have no choice but to follow.[11]

The drawing of object lessons from the private sphere and their application to the public sphere has proved to be hazardous. It is unlikely that municipal unions could follow a "whipsaw" strategy even if they wanted to. Municipal unions are most concerned with financial and personnel matters. Responsibility for these matters has not been delegated to the community school systems in Detroit and New York City. If one is forced to speculate, it is probable that only limited financial and personnel powers will be transferred to newly created neighborhood governments. Unions will continue to confine most of their bargaining efforts to the municipal level.

Kotler is convinced that where bureaucrats are entrenched in poor areas, as in Chicago, they will fight attempts to establish neighborhood governments:

> The amount of bureaucratic resistance will be an indicator of the extent of professional organization and resources of the social administration of the city. Where these are large, opposition will be great, and bureaucrats will forcefully oppose neighborhood claims for independent authority. . . . It must be anticipated that a bureaucracy will oppose neighborhood control with great re-

sources of money and heavy ideological attack, and will label the corporation a menace to democracy, efficiency, and quality. Bureaucratic opposition, and its implicit threat of a public employees' strike if a transfer proceeds, can exert great force and prevent political interests from supporting a transfer of authority to neighborhood corporations.[12]

Kotler's view of the position of bureaucrats toward neighborhood government is more realistic than Altshuler's. Experience with the campaign for community control of schools in New York City clearly indicates that white public employees and their organizations will strenuously oppose any form of neighborhood government unless it guarantees their job tenure and rights and the vesting of pension rights. Early retirement and transfer privileges would also alleviate bureaucratic opposition. The Detroit Federation of Teachers, for example, did not oppose the creation of a community school system because the enabling legislation safeguarded teachers' rights.

Liberals traditionally have been distrustful of local governments, which they contend are bastions of conservatism and reaction and intolerant of political dissent, and have worked to have the locus of decision making raised to Washington. They have supported integration and consequently oppose neighborhood government on the ground that it would be the legal embodiment of racial separatism and hence a form of segregation. Commencing in the late 1960's, however, some liberals began to support decentralization of decision making to the neighborhood level as a mechanism for transfering power to the powerless.

The hypothesis can be advanced that the best prospect for implementing a system of neighborhood government will be in a city where black voting strength is approaching a majority. Blacks generally appear to be in favor of creating such a system, and it may receive growing white support with the passage of time for five primary reasons. (1) Whites may become convinced that neighborhood governments will relieve them of legal responsibility for helping the residents of black ghettos solve their problems. (2) Whites may perceive neighborhood government as a vehicle for the preservation of white control in certain neighborhoods in a city coming under black domination. (3) The creation of neighborhood governments would legitimize existing racial segregation and reduce pressures for busing of students and integration of housing and schools. (4) Whites may become convinced that the creation of neighborhood governments may transform black militants into moderate political leaders who will deal responsibly with city officials. (5) Wealthier neighborhoods might favor the creation of a system of neighborhood government for tax reasons. Residents might prefer to raise taxes for the benefit of their own neighborhoods instead of having the city raise taxes and spend much of the proceeds in ghetto areas.

A related hypothesis can be advanced that black interest in and support for the creation of a system of neighborhood government will decrease as blacks achieve majority status in a large city. Since the instruments of control probably will pass to blacks as they become the majority in the city, it is not unreasonable to conclude that blacks will have less interest in community control. Inferential evidence supporting this conclusion is found in a 1961 voting study of Cleveland that revealed a decline in black support for metropolitan reform as the black population increased.[13] On the other hand, a more recent study revealed that a majority of the blacks in Jacksonville, Florida, voted in favor of consolidating the city with Duval County, even though the consolidation resulted in the black population dropping from approximately 42 percent of the city's population to 23 percent of the total population of the consolidated city-county.[14]

Although we have advocated the formation of multipurpose ones, neighborhood governments are most apt to be based initially upon a single function—education in most instances. If this function is handled successfully, the neighborhood government may undergo a gradual metamorphosis into a multifunctional one by incrementally acquiring responsibility for additional functions.

The public has not displayed either strong support for or opposition to the administrative reforms introduced by mayors to improve city hall-neighborhood communications and the delivery of services on the neighborhood level. Nor has there been strong opposition on the part of the bureaucracy to these reforms. Even the most militant supporters of neighborhood government have not expressed opposition to the reforms beyond statements indicating that the reforms either are cooptative devices or tokenism. The movement for administrative reform appears to be gaining momentum in large cities, and it is not unreasonable to predict that this phase of the reform model will be the easiest to implement.

Although the unrepresentativeness of the city council in most large cities is readily apparent to all, no major movement has been launched for electoral reform. The use of proportional representation in community school board elections in New York City was not the product of popular demand for the institution of the system; rather, it was mandated by the state legislature to ensure that minorities would have direct representation on the community school boards. Of the electoral systems designed to provide minority representation, proportional representation is the preferable system; but opposition to it is so strong and emotional that it probably will not be widely adopted in the foreseeable future. Political support will be easier to mobilize for a return to district or ward elections, even though such a system will not provide representation in proportion to the voting strength of various groups and suffers from the disadvantages described in Chapter 4.

Concluding Comments

Emotional and ideological statements to the effect that city governments have failed to solve major problems and are ungovernable should not blind us to the fact that a number of large city governments have coped successfully with many major problems. We find that these governments have been open and responsive. They have anticipated problems and have initiated effective corrective action.

Most citizens in large cities appear to be interested only in the delivery of quality public services. As long as quality services are delivered on the neighborhood level in adequate amounts, the average citizen will be little interested in community control of governmental institutions and functions, administrative reform, or electoral reform. He will confine his civic activities to voting and an occasional protest against the inadequate delivery of a service or a major project threatening to disrupt his neighborhood—urban renewal or an expressway, for example. Only the atypical citizen will devote much time to civic activities when the local government is functioning efficiently, delivering the desired services, and providing the desired facilities.

To date, the demand for the establishment of a system of neighborhood government has come from individuals and organizations who charge the city government with failure to provide an adequate amount of quality services. Adoption of the institutional and electoral changes contained in our model will enable cities to cope more effectively with the urban malaise.

In conclusion, structural change and tinkering alone cannot solve the multitudinous problems of the poor in central cities. In combination with electoral reform and increased financial resources, structural change and administrative innovations can do much to restore consent of the governed in alienated neighborhoods and revitalize local government.

Notes

CHAPTER I

1. Milton Kotler, "Two Essays on the Neighborhood Corporation," in Joint Economic Committee's *Urban America: Goals and Problems* (Washington, D. C.: United States Government Printing Office, August 1967), p. 176.
2. *Ibid.*
3. *Modernizing Local Government* (New York: Committee for Economic Development, July 1966), p. 47.
4. *Reshaping Government in Metropolitan Areas* (New York: Committee for Economic Development, February 1970).
5. *Royal Commission on Local Government in England: 1966–1969. Vol. 1: Report* (London: Her Majesty's Stationery Office, June 1969), pp. 95–108.
6. James L. Sundquist and David W. Davis, *Making Federalism Work* (Washington, D. C.: The Brookings Institution, 1969), pp. 117–121.
7. Milton Kotler, "Two Essays on the Neighborhood Corporation," p. 180.
8. Alan A. Altshuler, *Community Control: The Black Demand for Participation in Large American Cities* (New York: Pegasus, 1970), p. 197.
9. *Ibid.*, p. 199.
10. *Fiscal Balance in the American Federal System, Vol. 2: Metropolitan Fiscal Disparities* (Washington, D. C.: Advisory Commission on Intergovernmental Relations, October 1967), p. 17.
11. Howard W. Hallman, *Community Corporations and Neighborhood Control* (Washington, D. C.: Center for Governmental Studies, 1970), p. 8.
12. Joseph F. Zimmerman, *The Massachusetts Town Meeting: A Tenacious Institution* (Albany: Graduate School of Public Affairs, State University of New York at Albany, 1967).
13. Milton Kotler, *Neighborhood Government* (Indianapolis: The Bobbs-Merrill Company, 1969), p. 85.
14. Howard W. Hallman, *Community Control: A Study of Community Corporations and Neighborhood Boards* (Washington, D. C.: Washington Center for Metropolitan Studies, October 1969), p. 30.
15. Kotler, *Neighborhood Government*, p. 64.
16. See *Performance of Urban Functions: Local and Areawide* (Washington, D. C.: Advisory Commission on Intergovernmental Relations, September 1963).

17. "Size Can Make a Difference—A Closer Look," *ACIR Information Bulletin,* September 16, 1970.
18. *Ibid.,* p. 8.
19. *Fiscal Balance,* pp. 16–17.

CHAPTER II

1. Leonard Buder, "Decentralization of Schools Is Considered Successful," *The New York Times,* July 1, 1971, p. 59.

CHAPTER III

1. Paul Dolan, "Pseudo-Ombudsmen," *National Civic Review,* July 1969, p. 299.
2. Randy H. Hamilton, "Can You Fight City Hall and Win?" *Public Management,* October 1967, p. 269.
3. *Ibid.,* p. 270.
4. Dolan, "Pseudo-Ombudsmen," p. 298.
5. "The Public: A Hard Line," *Newsweek,* March 8, 1971, p. 40.
6. *The New York Times,* September 27, 1965, p. 1.
7. National Commission on Urban Problems, *Building the American City* (Washington, D. C.: United States Government Printing Office, 1968), p. 351.
8. *Ibid.*
9. Elisha C. Freedman and Edward A. Lehan, " 'Modest Adventure' in Hartford," *Public Management,* May 1967, pp. 116–123.
10. Terrance C. Smith, "City Lawmakers Override Mayor on 32 City Halls," *The New York Times,* June 24, 1966, p. 1.
11. Carl W. Stenberg, *The New Grass Roots Government?* (Washington, D. C.: Advisory Commission on Intergovernmental Relations, 1972), p. 9.
12. *Resolution 24079,* Board of Supervisors, County of San Mateo, State of California.
13. *Revised Code of Washington,* chap. 35.10.
14. *City Government for the Future* (Los Angeles: Los Angeles City Charter Commission, July 1969), p. 19.
15. *Ibid.,* p. 129.
16. *The Government of Metropolitan Sacramento* (Chicago: Public Administration Service, 1957).
17. *Sub-Urbs in the City* (Minneapolis: The Citizens League, 1970).
18. *Building the American City,* p. 352.
19. *Ibid.*
20. *Ibid.,* pp. 350–351.
21. *Ibid.,* pp. 353–354.

CHAPTER IV

1. George E. Berkley, "Flaws in At-large Voting," *National Civic Review,* July 1966, p. 372.
2. *Kilgarlin v. Hill,* 386 U. S. 120 (1967).
3. *Owens v. School Committee of Boston,* 304 F. Supp. 1327 (1969).
4. Richard S. Childs, *The First 50 Years* (New York: National Municipal League, 1965), p. 37.
5. *Avery v. Midland County, Texas et al,* 390 U. S. 474 (1968).
6. *Dusch v. Davis,* 387 U. S. 112 (1967).
7. *Fortson v. Dorsey,* 379 U. S. 433 (1965).

8. *New York City Charter,* chap. 2, sec. 22 (1963).
9. *Opinion to the House of Representatives,* 21 R.I. 41 (1898).
10. *McArdle et al v. Mayor, etc. of City of Jersey City,* 66 N.J.L. 590 (1901).
11. *State ex rel. Bowden v. Bedell et al,* 68 N.J.L. 451 (1902).
12. *State ex rel. v. Constantine,* 42 O.S. 437 (1884).
13. *Reutener v. City of Cleveland,* 107 O.S. 117 (1923).
14. *Blaikie v. Power,* 243 N.Y.S. 2d 185, 193 N.E. 2d 55.
15. *Blaikie v. Power,* 375 U. S. 439 (1964).
16. *Reynolds v. Sims,* 377 U. S. 533 (1964).
17. *Avery v. Midland County, Texas et al,* 390 U. S. 474 (1968).
18. *Constitution of the State of Illinois,* art. 4, sec. 7.
19. *People v. Strassheim,* 240 Ill. 279 (1909).
20. *Illinois Revised Statutes,* chap. 46, art. 8, sec. 13 (1965).
21. George S. Blair, *Cumulative Voting: An Effective Electoral Device in Illinois Politics* (Urbana: The University of Illinois Press, 1960), pp. 103–104.
22. Belle Zeller and Hugh A. Bone, "The Repeal of P.R. in New York City: Ten Years in Retrospect," *The American Political Science Review,* December 1948, p. 1127.
23. George H. Hallett, Jr., *Proportional Representation: The Key to Democracy* (New York: National Municipal League, 1940), pp. 72–73.
24. *Ibid.,* p. 57.

CHAPTER V

1. Milton Kotler, *Neighborhood Government* (Indianapolis: The Bobbs-Merrill Company, 1969), pp. 82–85.
2. Daniel P. Moynihan, "The New Racialism," *The Atlantic Monthly,* August 1968, p. 38.
3. Alan A. Altshuler, *Community Control: The Black Demand for Participation in Large American Cities* (New York: Pegasus, 1970), pp. 200–207.
4. Carl W. Stenberg, *The New Grass Roots Government?* (Washington, D. C.: Advisory Commission on Intergovernmental Relations, 1972), p. 16.
5. Kotler, *Neighborhood Government,* p. 35.
6. *Ibid.,* pp. 35–36.
7. *Ibid.,* p. 36.
8. Howard W. Hallman, *Administrative Decentralization and Citizen Control* (Washington, D. C.: Center for Governmental Studies, March 1971), p. 8.
9. "Mayor LaGuardia on P.R.," *National Municipal Review,* April 1940, p. 275.
10. Milton Kotler, "Two Essays on the Neighborhood Corporation," in Joint Economic Committee's *Urban America: Goals and Problems* (Washington, D. C.: United States Government Printing Office, August 1967), p. 181.
11. Altshuler, *Community Control,* p. 118.
12. Kotler, *Neighborhood Government,* p. 70.
13. Richard A. Watson and John H. Romani, "Metropolitan Government for Metropolitan Cleveland: An Analysis of the Voting Records," *Midwest Journal of Political Science,* November 1961, pp. 365–390.
14. Joseph F. Zimmerman, "Metropolitan Reform in the U. S.: An Overview," *Public Administration Review,* September/October 1970, pp. 537–538.

Bibliography

BOOKS, MONOGRAPHS, AND REPORTS

Advisory Commission on Intergovernmental Relations. *Urban and Rural America: Policies for Future Growth.* Washington, D. C.: United States Government Printing Office, April 1968.

Almond, Gabriel, and Sidney Verba. *The Civic Culture.* Princeton: Princeton University Press, 1963.

Altshuler, Alan A. *Community Control: The Black Demand for Participation in Large American Cities.* New York: Pegasus, 1970.

Analysis of Elections for Community School Boards. New York: United Parents Association, 1970. Mimeographed.

Banfield, Edward C. *The Unheavenly City.* Boston: Little, Brown and Company, 1970.

Banfield, Edward C., and James Q. Wilson. *City Politics.* Cambridge: Harvard University Press and the M.I.T. Press, 1963.

Bebout, John E. *Decentralization and the City Charter.* Lansing. Citizens Research Council of Michigan, August 1971.

Benson, Charles S., and Peter B. Lund. *Neighborhood Distribution of Local Public Services.* Berkeley: Institute of Governmental Studies, University of California, 1969.

Blair, George S. *Cumulative Voting: An Effective Electoral Device in Illinois Politics.* Urbana: The University of Illinois Press, 1960.

Blecher, Earl M. *Advocacy Planning for Urban Development.* New York: Praeger Publishers, 1971.

Bridging the Gulf. New York: Citizens Union, June 24, 1970.

CDCs: New Hope for the Inner City. New York: The Twentieth Century Fund, 1971.

Center for Policy Analysis, *The Mayor and Model Cities.* Washington, D. C.: National League of Cities and the United States Conference of Mayors, 1972.

Childs, Richard S. *The First 50 Years,* New York: National Municipal League, 1965.

Citizen Participation in Model Cities: A HUD Guide. Washington, D. C.: United States Department of Housing and Urban Development, December 1968.

Citizen Participation Today: Proceedings of a Staff Conference. Chicago: United States Department of Housing and Urban Development, Region IV, August 1968.

City Government for the Future. Los Angeles: Los Angeles City Charter Commission, July 1969.

The Committee on Municipal Affairs and The Committee on Labor and Social Security Legislation, *The New York City School Decentralization Law and Its Effect on Collective Bargaining.* New York: The Association of the Bar of the City of New York, 1972.

Community Participation in Public Elementary Schools: A Survey Report. Washington, D. C.: Center for Governmental Studies, 1970.

Community Planning Districts. New York: City Planning Commission, March 1968.

Connery, Robert H., ed. Urban Riots: *Violence and Social Change.* New York: The Academy of Political Science, 1968.

Cumulative Voting. Chicago: League of Women Voters of Illinois, June 1969.

Dahl, Robert A. *Who Governs?* New Haven: Yale University Press, 1961.

Demas, Boulton H. *The School Elections: A Critique of the 1969 New York City School Decentralization.* New York: Institute for Community Studies, Queens College, 1971.

A Discussion Draft for the Symposium on Decentralizing New York City Government. New York: The Association of the Bar of the City of New York, 1970.

Easton, David. *A Systems Analysis of Political Life.* New York: John Wiley & Sons, Inc., 1965.

Fein, Leonard J. *The Ecology of the Public Schools: An Inquiry into Community Control.* Indianapolis: The Bobbs-Merrill Company, Inc., 1972.

Fesler, James W. *Area and Administration.* University: University of Alabama Press, 1949.

Financial Problems in the Detroit School District. Detroit: Citizens Research Council of Michigan, February 1972.

Fiscal Balance in the American Federal System, Vol. 2: Metropolitan Fiscal Disparities. Washington, D. C.: Advisory Commission on Intergovernmental Relations, October 1967.

Gellhorn, Walter. *When Americans Complain: Governmental Grievance Procedures.* Cambridge: Harvard University Press, 1966.

Gittell, Marilyn. *Participants and Participation: A Study of School Policy in New York City.* New York: Center for Urban Education, 1967.

Gittell, Marilyn, and T. Edward Hollander. *Six Urban School Districts: A Comparative Study of Institutional Response.* New York: Praeger Publishers, 1968.

Gittell, Marilyn. *et al. Demonstration for Social Change: An Experiment in Local Control.* New York: Institute for Community Studies, Queens College, 1971.

The Government of Metropolitan Sacramento. Chicago: Public Administration Service, 1957.

Guidelines for Regional and Central Boards of Education. Detroit: Board of Education, 1970.

Haddad, William F., and G. Douglas Pugh, eds. *Black Economic Development.* Englewood Cliffs, N. J.: Prentice-Hall, Inc., 1969.

Hallett, George H., Jr. *Proportional Representation: The Key to Democracy.* New York: National Municipal League, 1940.

Hallman, Howard W. *Community Control: A Study of Community Corporations and Neighborhood Boards.* Washington, D. C.: Washington Center for Metropolitan Studies, October 1969.

Hallman, Howard W. *Community Corporations and Neighborhood Control.* Washington, D. C.: Center for Governmental Studies, 1970.

Hallman, Howard W. *Elements of a Local System for the Delivery of Manpower Services,* Washington, D. C.: Center for Governmental Studies, 1970.

Haugen, Rolf N. B., ed. *Report of the Northern New England Assembly on The Ombudsman: Citizen Protector.* Burlington: Government Research Center, University of Vermont, Fall, 1969.

Hunter, Floyd. *Community Power Structure: A Study of Decisionmakers.* Chapel Hill: The University of North Carolina Press, 1953.

Joint Economic Committee, *Employment and Manpower Problems in the Cities: Implications of the Report of the National Advisory Commission on Civil Disorders.* Washington, D. C.: United States Government Printing Office, 1968.

Keller, Suzanne. *The Urban Neighborhood.* New York: Random House, 1968.

The Kerner Report Revisited. Urbana: Institute of Government and Public Affairs, June 1970.

Kotler, Milton. *Neighborhood Government.* Indianapolis: The Bobbs-Merrill Company, 1969.

Lakeman, Enid. *How Democracies Vote.* London: Faber and Faber, 1970.

Levin, Henry M., ed. *Community Control of Schools.* Washington, D. C.: The Brookings Institution, 1970.

Levin, Murray B. *The Alienated Voter.* New York: Holt, Rinehart and Winston, Inc., 1960.

Levine, Naomi. *Schools in Crisis.* New York: Popular Library, 1969.

Lipsky, Michael. *Protest in City Politics: Rent Strikes, Housing and the Power of the Poor.* Chicago: Rand McNally & Company, 1970.

Marshall Kaplan, Gans, and Kahn. *The Model Cities Program.* New York: Praeger Publishers, 1970.

McMurrin, Sterling M., ed. *Resources for Urban Schools: Better Use and Balance.* New York: Committee for Economic Development, 1971.

Merton, Robert K. *Social Theory and Social Structure.* Rev. ed. New York: The Free Press, 1957.

Model Cities: A Report on Progress. Washington, D. C.: National League of Cities and the United States Conference of Mayors, 1971.

Model City Charter. 6th ed. New York: National Municipal League, 1964.

Modernizing Local Government. New York: Committee for Economic Development, July 1966.

Moynihan, Daniel P. *Maximum Feasible Misunderstanding.* New York: The Free Press, 1969.

National Commission on Urban Problems. *Building the American City.* Washington, D. C.: United States Government Printing Office, 1968.

Neighborhood Facilities and Municipal Decentralization: Volume II—Case Studies of Twelve Cities. Washington, D. C.: Center for Governmental Studies, 1971.

One Year Later. New York: Urban America, Inc., 1969.

Performance of Urban Functions: Local and Areawide. Washington, D. C.: Advisory Commission on Intergovernmental Relations, September 1963.

Polsby, Nelson W. *Community Power and Political Theory.* New Haven: Yale University Press, 1963.

Proceedings of a Conference on Public Administration and Neighborhood Control. Washington, D. C.: Center for Governmental Studies, 1970.

A Program for Community Districts. New York: Citizens Union and Citizens Housing and Planning Council, June 1964.

Rae, Douglas. *The Political Consequences of Electoral Laws.* New Haven: Yale University Press, 1967.

Reconnection for Learning: A Community School System for New York City. New York: Mayor's Advisory Panel on Decentralization of the New York City Schools, 1967.

Report for Action. Trenton, N. J.: Governor's Select Commission on Civil Disorder, February 1968.

Report of the National Advisory Commission on Civil Disorders. Washington, D. C.: United States Government Printing Office, 1968.

Reshaping Government in Metropolitan Areas. New York: Committee for Economic Development, February 1970.

Rogers, David. 110 Livingston Street. New York: Random House, Inc., 1968.

Royal Commission on Local Government in England: 1966–1969. Vol. I: Report. London: Her Majesty's Stationery Office, June 1969.

Shalala, Donna E. Neighborhood Governance: Issues and Proposals. New York: The American Jewish Committee, 1971.

Smiley, Marjorie, and Harry L. Miller, eds. Policy Issues in Urban Education. New York: The Free Press, 1968.

Spiegel, Hans B. C., ed. Citizen Participation in Urban Development. Vol. I: Concepts and Issues. Washington, D. C.: Center for Community Studies, NTL Institute for Applied Behavioral Science, 1968.

Spiegel, Hans B. C., et al. Neighborhood Power and Control Implication for Urban Planning. Springfield, Va., Clearinghouse for Federal Scientific and Technical Clearinghouse, November 1968.

Stenberg, Carl W. The New Grass Roots Government? Washington, D. C.: Advisory Commission on Intergovernmental Relations, 1972.

Sub-Urbs in the City. Minneapolis: The Citizens League, 1970.

Sundquist, James L., and David W. Davis. Making Federalism Work. Washington, D. C.: The Brookings Institution, 1969.

Supplemental Studies for The National Advisory Commission on Civil Disorders. Washington, D. C.: United States Government Printing Office, 1968.

Syed, Anwar. The Political Theory of American Local Government. New York: Random House, Inc., 1966.

Task Force on Jurisdiction and Structure, Re-Structuring the Government of New York City. New York: State Study Commission for New York City, 1972.

The Twentieth Century Fund Task Force on Employment Problems of Black Youth. The Job Crisis for Black Youth. New York: Praeger Publishers, 1971.

Violence in the City—An End or a Beginning? Los Angeles: The Governor's Commission on the Los Angeles Riots, 1965.

Washnis, George J. Little City Halls. Washington, D. C.: Center for Governmental Studies, 1971.

Watson, Nelson A., and James W. Sterling. Police and Their Opinions. Washington, D. C.: International Chiefs of Police, 1969.

Zimmerman, Joseph F. The Massachusetts Town Meeting: A Tenacious Institution. Albany: Graduate School of Public Affairs, State University of New York at Albany, 1967.

ARTICLES

Aberbach, Joel D. "Alienation and Political Behavior." The American Political Science Review, March 1969, pp. 86–99.

Aberbach, Joel D., and Jack L. Walker. "The Meanings of Black Power: A Comparison of White and Black Interpretations of a Political Slogan." The American Political Science Review, June 1970, pp. 367–388.

Aleshire, Robert A. "Organizing for Neighborhood Management: Drawing on the Federal Experience." Public Management, January 1971, pp. 7–9.

Alford, Robert R., and Eugene C. Lee. "Voting Turnout in American Cities." The American Political Science Review, September 1968, pp. 796–813.

Aronowitz, Stanley. "The Dialectics of Community Control." Social Policy, May/June 1970, pp. 47–51.

Berkley, George E. "Flaws in At-Large Voting." *National Civic Review,* July 1966, pp. 370–373, 379.

Bloombaum, Milton. "The Conditions Underlying Race Riots as Portrayed by Multidimensional Scalogram Analysis: A Reanalysis of Lieberson and Silverman's Data." *The American Sociological Review,* February 1968, pp. 76–91.

Callahan, John, and Donna E. Shalala. "Some Fiscal Dimensions of Three Hypothetical Decentralization Plans." *Education and Urban Society,* November 1969, pp. 40–53.

Cohen, David K. "The Price of Community Control." *Commentary,* July 1969, pp. 23–32.

Cohn, Jules. "Business and the Hard-Core Unemployed: Promise and Performance." *Social Policy,* May/June 1970, pp. 56–60.

"Community Economic Development, Part 1." *Law and Contemporary Problems,* Winter 1971, entire issue.

Condlin, Robert J. "Citizens, Police, and Polarization: Are Perceptions More Important than Facts?" *Journal of Urban Law,* Vol. 47, No. 3, 1969–1970, pp. 653–672.

Dahl, Robert A. "The City in the Future of Democracy." *The American Political Science Review,* December 1967, pp. 953–970.

Dennis, Jack. "Support for the Institution of Elections by the Mass Public." *The American Political Science Review,* September 1970, pp. 819–835.

Dolan, Paul. "Pseudo-Ombudsmen." *National Civic Review,* July 1969, pp. 297–301, 306.

Ferman, Louis A., ed. "Evaluating the War on Poverty." *The Annals,* September 1969, entire issue.

Fesler, James W. "Approaches to the Understanding of Decentralization." *The Journal of Politics,* August 1965, pp. 536–566.

Finifter, Ada W. "Dimensions of Political Alienation." *The American Political Science Review,* June 1970, pp. 389–410.

Freedman, Elisha C., and Edward A. Lehan. " 'Modest Adventure' in Hartford." *Public Management,* May 1967, pp. 116–123.

Gittell, Marilyn. "Community Control of Education." In Robert H. Connery, ed., *Urban Riots: Violence and Social Change,* pp. 60–71. New York: The Academy of Political Science, 1968.

Gittell, Marilyn. "The Community School in the Nation." *Community Issues,* February 1970, entire issue.

Gittell, Marilyn. "School Decentralization Today." *Community,* November 1971, pp. 1–4.

Glazer, Nathan. "For White and Black, Community Control Is the Issue." *The New York Times Magazine,* April 27, 1969, pp. 36–54.

Gottfried, Frances. "A Survey of Parental Views of the Ocean Hill-Brownsville Experiment." *Community Issues,* October 1970, entire issue.

Grollman, Judith E. "Decentralization of Municipal Services." *Urban Data Service Reports,* February 1971.

Hallman, Howard W. "Guidelines for Neighborhood Management." *Public Management,* January 1971, pp. 3–5.

Hamilton, Randy H. "Can You Fight City Hall and Win?" *Public Management,* October 1967, pp. 268–275.

Harris, Joseph P. "The Practical Workings of Proportional Representation in the United States and Canada." *National Municipal Review,* May 1930, pp. 337–383.

Hechinger, Fred M. "The Changing City: School Turmoil." *The New York Times,* June 6, 1969, p. 1.

"Home Town in the Great City." *The Searchlight,* July 1947, pp. 1–8.

Inkeles, Alex. "Participant Citizenship in Six Developing Countries." *The American Political Science Review,* December 1969, pp. 1120–1141.

Kotler, Milton. "Two Essays on the Neighborhood Corporation." In Joint Economic Committee's *Urban America: Goals and Problems*, pp. 170–191. Washington, D. C.: United States Government Printing Office, August 1967.

Kristol, Irving. "Decentralization for What?" *The Public Interest*, Spring 1968, pp. 17–25.

Lawer, Neil. "Boston's Little City Hall Program." *Public Administration Review*, July/August 1971, pp. 456–457.

Lieberson, Stanley, and Arnold R. Silverman. "The Precipitants and Underlying Conditions of Race Riots." *The American Sociological Review*, December 1965, pp. 887–898.

Lineberry, Robert L., and Edmund P. Fowler. "Reformism and Public Policies in American Cities." *The American Political Science Review*, September 1967, pp. 701–716.

Lupsha, Peter A. "On Theories of Urban Violence." *Urban Affairs Quarterly*, March 1969, pp. 273–296.

Masoti, Louis H., ed. "Urban Violence and Disorder." *American Behavioral Scientist*, March-April 1968, entire issue.

McBain, Howard L. "Proportional Representation in American Cities." *Political Science Quarterly*, June 1922, pp. 281–298.

Merelman, Richard M. "On the Neo-Elitist Critique of Community Power." *The American Political Science Review*, June 1968, pp. 451–460.

Miller, S. M., and Martin Rein. "Participation, Poverty, and Administration." *Public Administration Review*, January-February 1969, pp. 15–25.

Moley, Raymond. "Proportional Representation in Cleveland." *Political Science Quarterly*, December 1923, pp. 652–669.

Moley, Raymond. "Representation in Dayton and Ashtabula." *National Municipal Review*, January 1918, pp. 27–35.

Moore, Charles H., and Ray E. Johnston. "School Decentralization and the Politics of Public Education." *Urban Affairs Quarterly*, June 1971, pp. 421–446.

Mott, Rodney L. "Invalid Ballots Under the Hare System of Proportional Representation." *The American Political Science Review*, November 1926, pp. 874–882.

Moynihan, Daniel P. "The New Racialism." *The Atlantic Monthly*, August 1968, pp. 35–40.

Neal, Arthur G., and Salomon Rettig. "On the Multidimensionality of Alienation." *The American Sociological Review*, February 1967, pp. 54–64.

Oliver, James B., Jr. "Norfolk Gets More Citizens Involved with Town Hall Meetings." *Virginia Town & City*, July 1970, pp. 5–7.

Parsons, Tim. "The Community School Movement." *Community Issues*, December 1970, entire issue.

Participation of the Poor in the Community Decision-making Process. Washington, D. C.: Office of Economic Opportunity, August 1969.

Peterson, Paul E. "Forms of Representation: Participation of the Poor in the Community Action Program." *The American Political Science Review*, June 1970, pp. 491–507.

Reichler, Oxie. "The Politician Hates P.R." *National Municipal Review*, June 1947, pp. 316–320.

Riessman, Frank, and Alan Gartner. "Community Control and Radical Social Change." *Social Policy*, May/June 1970, pp. 52–55.

Scher, Richard K. "Decentralization and the New York State Legislature." *The Urban Review*, September 1969, pp. 13–19.

"Size Can Make a Difference—A Closer Look." *ACIR Information Bulletin*, September 16, 1970.

Skjei, Stephen S. "Urban Systems Advocacy." *Journal of The American Institute of Planners*, January 1972, pp. 11–24.

Smith, Terrance C. "City Lawmakers Override Mayor on 32 City Halls." *The New York Times,* June 24, 1966, p. 1.

Spier, Adele. "Two Bridges Model School District: A Profile." *Community Issues,* February 1969, entire issue.

Stein, Andrew. "Government for New York's Communities." Published by the author, a New York State Assemblyman, September 1971.

Stenberg, Carl W. "Citizens and the Administrative State: From Participation to Power." *Public Administration Review,* May/June 1972, pp. 190–197.

Stenberg, Carl W. "Decentralization and the City." *In 1972 Municipal Year Book,* pp. 88–96. Washington, D. C.: International City Management Association, 1972.

Stenberg, Carl W. "The History and Future of Citizen Participation: An Overview." An address presented at the 1971 National Conference on Public Administration, Denver, Colorado, April 19, 1971.

Sterzer, Earl E. "Neighborhood Grant Program Lets Citizens Decide." *Public Management,* January 1971, pp. 10–11.

Tomlinson, T. M. "The Development of a Riot Ideology Among Urban Negroes. *American Behavioral Scientist,* March-April 1968, pp. 27–31.

Watson, Richard A., and John H. Romani. "Metropolitan Government for Metropolitan Cleveland: An Analysis of the Voting Records." *Midwest Journal of Political Science,* November 1961, pp. 365–390.

Weaver, Leon H. "Representation of Minorities in At-Large Elections in City and Village Governments Under Michigan Law." *Journal of Urban Law,* August 1971, pp. 131–161.

Wilson, Kenneth D. "Neighborhood Proposal Aimed at Citizen Participation." *Public Management,* January 1971, pp. 12–13.

Zeller, Belle, and Hugh A. Bone. "The Repeal of P. R. in New York City: Ten Years in Retrospect." *The American Political Science Review,* December 1948, pp. 1127–1148.

Zimmerman, Joseph F. "Community Building in Large Cities." *Administration,* Summer 1972, pp. 71–87.

Zimmerman, Joseph F. "Electoral Reform Needed to End Political Alienation." *National Civic Review,* January 1971, pp. 6–10, 21.

Zimmerman, Joseph F. "Heading Off City Hall-Neighborhood Wars. *Nation's Cities,* November 1970, pp. 18–21, 39.

Zimmerman, Joseph F. "Metropolitan Reform in the U. S.: An Overview." *Public Administration Review,* September/October 1970, pp. 531–543.

Zimmerman, Joseph F. "Neighborhood Governments: Goal of New Municipal Reformers." *Connecticut Government,* Summer 1971, pp. 1–4.

Zimmerman, Joseph F. "Neighborhoods and Citizen Involvement." *Public Administration Review,* May/June 1972, pp. 201–210.

Zimmerman, Joseph F. "The Politics of Neighborhood Government." *Studies in Comparative Local Government,* Summer 1971, pp. 28–39.

Zwiebach, Burton. "Democratic Theory and Community Control." *Community Issues,* March 1969, entire issue.

Index

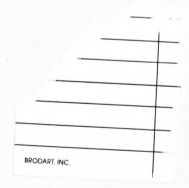

BRODART, INC.